"Dr Bajpai brings a rare blend of research, lived experience, and reflection to a question that matters deeply in today's world—how do we keep coaching real, connected, and empathetic in today's digital age? This book offers both a clear-eyed analysis and a hopeful vision for the future, reminding us that while technology may transform how we coach, it is our humanity that gives coaching its transformational power".

Marshall Goldsmith *is the Thinkers50 #1 Executive Coach and New York Times bestselling author of* The Earned Life, Triggers, *and* What Got You Here Won't Get You There

"Digital Coaching has become the standard mode for coach delivery for both personal and organisational coaching. Understanding the what, how and the why are essential skills for coaches in the digital age. This book provides answers to these questions for the modern coach".

Jonathan Passmore *is the Professor of Coaching & Behavioural Change at Henley Business School, UK*

"This book is a fascinating journey through the most significant transformation of our world and the impact this has had and will have on the role of the executive coach. The book has emerged largely from the author's doctoral thesis and certainly it contains a fascinating wealth of research data – his own and others'. But it is also an engaging and accessible story. From the very start Brajesh Bajpai invites the reader to join him as he lays out the digital landscape we live and work in, reminds us of what we already know and do that is digital and points the way to how our coaching might become most relevant to today's leaders. With masses of vignettes and examples, quotes and reflective exercises, he never loses the 'human' and indeed he succeeds in fulfilling the aspiration of Marcel Proust: 'The real voyage of discovery consists not in seeking new landscapes, but in having new eyes'".

Professor Charlotte Sills, *coach, psychotherapist, supervisor and Professor of Coaching at Hult Ashridge Executive Education*

"In a time when technology is rewriting how organisations connect, learn, and lead, Brajesh's *Coaching in the Digital Age* arrives as a vital contribution. It bridges the worlds of research and practice to show how coaching can be a lever for digital transformation, grounded in humanity, ethics, and purpose. For CHROs and senior HR leaders, it offers fresh perspectives on building resilience, empathy, and trust across distributed teams. Brajesh brings the rare clarity of a practitioner-scholar, helping organisations harness coaching not just as a tool for leaders, but as a catalyst for organisational renewal".

Ronald Schellekens, *Global CHRO of Magnum Ice Cream, member of the Supervisory Board at Staffbase*

"In *Coaching in the Digital Age*, Brajesh succeeds in what many attempt but few achieve, to bridge the lived reality of coaching practice with the reflective depth of doctoral research. Drawing on a constructivist lens and rich practitioner inquiry, he illuminates how digitalisation is reshaping not just the tools and contexts of coaching, but the very essence of presence, empathy, and connection. This work is particularly significant for those of us engaged in developing coach scholars. It offers a model of how rigorous, reflexive research can speak meaningfully to practitioners while advancing our collective understanding of coaching as a social and relational practice. Brajesh's 4-Winged Framework and reflections on digital presence add new vocabulary and conceptual clarity to a rapidly evolving field. *Coaching in the Digital Age* will stand as an important text for coaches, researchers, and supervisors seeking to make sense of what it means to coach, and to be human, in a digitally mediated world".

Judie Gannon, *Director of Doctoral Programmes at the Oxford Brookes Business School, UK, and a teacher and supervisor on the Doctorate in Coaching & Mentoring Program*

"Coaching today stands at the intersection of technology and humanity. Dr Bajpai brings the rigour of research and the wisdom of experience to examine how digitalisation, AI, and virtual presence are reshaping what it means to coach and to lead. This book doesn't lament change, it humanises it. With clarity and empathy, it helps coaches, leaders, and organisations navigate the shifting boundaries between the human and the digital. In doing so, it reminds us that while technology may transform our methods, it is our curiosity, compassion, and connection that will always define our impact".

Harit Nagpal, *MD and CEO, Tata Play Ltd, and author of* Adapt: To Thrive, Not Just Survive *and* Pivot: Between Two Options, Pick the Third

"Like it or not, coaching today is a digital activity. Day-to-day interactions in organisations increasingly involve AI and other digital technologies. While not all coaches are working in virtual reality or partnered with an AI, every coach has to be as digitally competent as the clients they support. Maintaining presence and using intuition become much harder in a digital dialogue. To stay ahead, coaches must first engage with complexity, becoming systems literate, so they are able to coach the system, rather than just the client. They must become more mature, using more of their own wisdom to support clients in becoming wiser. And they must embrace the technology, creating partnerships that meld the competencies of both human and machine. This book provides practical guidance on how to embrace and capitalise on the rapidly evolving technology".

David Clutterbuck, *Visiting Professor at Henley Business School, UK, and Special Ambassador for the European Mentoring and Coaching Council*

"*Coaching in the Digital Age* is a timely and insightful contribution to the coaching and leadership development landscape. Brajesh brings together his deep practitioner experience and academic rigour to explore how digitalisation is reshaping the way we learn, lead and connect. His frameworks and reflections on digital presence, empathy, and human connection provide an eclectic mix and practical guidance for coaches and leaders/managers, as we navigate today's hybrid workplaces and other workforce developments. Importantly, I found *Coaching in the Digital Age* both relatable and thought-provoking. The book goes beyond coaching, it serves as a powerful resource for managers seeking to lead with authenticity and awareness, in a world increasingly mediated by technology. It captures the essence of what it means to remain deeply human even in times of digital transformation".

Ashok Ramchandran, *Director of Human Resources at the Aditya Birla Group (ABG)*

"This book is an essential read for any coaches navigating the evolving landscape of virtual coaching. Drawing on rigorous doctoral research conducted during the transformative pandemic period, it captures the pulse of a rapidly changing industry with authenticity and depth. With nearly three decades of industry experience, including 15 years as a coach and over a decade of academic research, Dr Bajpai integrates real-world coaching examples and leadership challenges with practical, research-backed guidance. The result is a highly actionable roadmap for coaches seeking to elevate their practice and make a meaningful impact. Whether you're a seasoned practitioner or just beginning your journey, this book offers clear, immediately applicable strategies to thrive in any digital setting".

Elaine Cox, *Honorary Research Fellow, Oxford Brookes University, UK, and Founding Editor of the* International Journal of Evidence-Based Coaching and Mentoring

Coaching in the Digital Age

In a world where digitalisation and artificial intelligence are reshaping every aspect of work and life, *Coaching in the Digital Age* equips readers with the tools, strategies, and insights they need to thrive.

Drawing on the author's extensive research and lived experience across multiple countries, and working with over 500 senior coaching clients, this book offers a practical roadmap for navigating the challenges of virtual coaching while embracing the opportunities of a tech-driven future. With its unique 4-Winged Framework, actionable tips, and real-world examples, it empowers coaches to maintain their humanity, presence, and impact when navigating an increasingly digital world. From the blurred boundaries of virtual environments to the lessons learned during the COVID-19 era, this book delves into the complexities of coaching in a hybrid landscape. It provides essential guidance on digital transformation, virtual presence, and the evolving role of empathy and connection in coaching. Packed with ready-to-use strategies that will allow readers to upskill, adapt, and lead with authenticity whilst staying ahead in a rapidly changing industry.

Coaching in the Digital Age is an essential resource for executive coaches, coaching researchers, and those in coach training programmes. It is also a powerful guide for leaders and HR professionals seeking to foster resilience, trust, and human connection in their organisations.

Dr Brajesh Bajpai is an accredited Executive Coach with coaching degrees from the University of Cambridge, Ashridge (HULT), UK, and a Doctorate in Coaching and Mentoring from Oxford Brookes University, UK, who over the last 15 years has coached more than 500 clients across 30 countries.

Coaching in the Digital Age

A Practical Guide

Dr Brajesh Bajpai

LONDON AND NEW YORK

Designed cover image: Sankai via Getty Images

First published 2027
by Routledge
4 Park Square, Milton Park, Abingdon, Oxon OX14 4RN

and by Routledge
605 Third Avenue, New York, NY 10158

Routledge is an imprint of the Taylor & Francis Group, an informa business

AI Declaration: The ideas, structure, and arguments are entirely original and author-verified. The AI tools ChatGPT 4-o and Gemini 2.0 were used to refine phrasing and support proofreading.

British Library Cataloguing-in-Publication Data
A catalogue record for this book is available from the British Library

ISBN: 978-1-041-07105-1 (hbk)
ISBN: 978-1-041-07103-7 (pbk)
ISBN: 978-1-003-63883-4 (ebk)

DOI: 10.4324/9781003638834

Typeset in Sabon
by SPi Technologies India Pvt Ltd (Straive)

Contents

Illustrations

Figures

Tables

Reflective Exercises

About the Author

Dr Brajesh Bajpai is an accredited executive coach (EMCC Senior Practitioner) and holds a doctorate in Coaching and Mentoring from Oxford Brookes University. He also holds a Coaching Diploma from the University of Cambridge and an MSc in Executive Coaching, along with additional coaching accreditation from Ashridge (HULT International Business School).

Alongside his academic work across internationally reputed institutions, Brajesh has spent over 15 years working as an executive coach and developmental partner to more than 500 clients across diverse industries in over 30 countries.

He is the founder of The Coaching Project, an India-based initiative committed to advancing ethical, research-informed, and evidence-based executive coaching aligned with global best practices. Brajesh regularly presents at international coaching conferences and is invited to academic and practitioner podcasts to share his research and coaching practice. Between 2016 and 2019, he was selected as a coach and advisory mentor for the Queen's Young Leaders Program.

In parallel, Brajesh brings nearly three decades of professional experience across three industries. His leadership roles in sales, marketing, and general management with organisations including PepsiCo, Frito-Lay, Marico, Vodafone, and Vodacom have taken him across 16 cities in five countries and three continents. He currently lives in Pune, India, with his wife and two cats, and continues to remain deeply engaged in coaching research, leadership development, wildlife conservation, writing, and exploring the world. In addition, Brajesh is helping build Nayanta, a new liberal arts university in India, as a member of its founding team.

Acknowledgements

My first and deepest thanks go to the **respondents** who graciously agreed to be interviewed for my research. For reasons of academic ethics, they must remain unnamed, but the appendix at the end of this book offers a brief portrait of these exceptionally busy and accomplished coaches who gave me the precious gift of their undivided attention and time. Without their openness and generosity, neither this research nor the book it inspired would have been possible. Thank you, **colleagues**,you know who you are.

My next thanks go to all my **coaching clients**, more than 500 of them, who, over the past 15 years, have enriched me through every session and every conversation. Your trust, honesty, and courage to reflect and grow have been my greatest teachers.

I extend my sincere thanks to the team at **Routledge UK**, who introduced me to the world of publishing and guided me through the many challenges of bringing my first book to life. I am especially grateful to my commissioning editor, **Katie Randal**, who initiated the project and later handed it over to **Sophie Ganesh** and onwards to **Maddie Gray** and **Rachel Cronin** during the production stage. My appreciation also goes to **Manon Berset** for her continued support and to **Tom Bedford** for supporting me during copyediting. To the entire team at **Routledge**: thank you for making my first experience as an author so rewarding and for your meticulous care at every stage.

Although I have already thanked my research supervisors, **Dr. Judie Gannon, Dr Elaine Cox, Dr Christian Ehrlich, Dr Guy Huber**, and the entire team at **Oxford Brookes University** in my thesis, they all deserve another heartfelt mention. This book stands firmly on the foundation of the research they so thoughtfully guided and supported.

Nothing I do could ever be completed, or be worth doing, without the unconditional love of **Karishma (Kim) Pais** and the steadfast support of **Brandy** and **Bailey**. This book has been no exception. Between changing countries, relocating homes, unpacking decade-old boxes, setting up a new base, managing Brandy and Bailey's first-ever flights, and navigating my own transition from industry to academia, the story of how this book came to life could easily fill another volume. Through it all, the constant thread,and the essential ingredient in all the chaos,has been the love of the three most important beings in my life. Their presence is my grounding, my joy, and my quiet reminder of what truly matters.

A heartfelt thank you to my **family** and **friends** who cheered me on from near and far. You smiled, sometimes sighed, and often endured my long stretches of absence and distraction, yet never stopped wishing me well. Kim and I continue to draw strength from the unwavering love and support of our **families**—our **parents**, **sisters**, **brothers**, **in-laws**, and my ever-encouraging **maternal clan**. Your patience, faith, and warmth have been the quiet rhythm behind this journey and a true source of its completion.

Preface

The Research Foundations of This Book

When Alice in Wonderland asked the cat which way to walk, the cat replied, "That depends a good deal on where you want to get to" (Carroll, 1992, p. 63). Similarly, good research is often constructed on the foundation of strong research questions. And so, rather than rushing into a methodology or getting lost in literature, I had started my research with the simplest yet most vital question: What do I really want to understand by the end of this research? I knew I wanted to *explore*, not *evaluate*. This wasn't about *proving* or *measuring*, but about *making sense* of what was unfolding in real time for coaches navigating a rapidly digitising world. That's why my central question avoided the tidy confines of "when", "where" or "who", and instead asked "how" and "what". From there, the aims, objectives, and subsidiary questions followed. The entire research was guided by a golden thread of a core question: **How are executive coaches dealing with the impact of digitalisation?**

For readers, especially researchers or doctoral candidates,who wish to engage more deeply with the academic architecture underpinning this book, including the research aims and objectives, my full doctoral thesis is available through Oxford Brookes University (Bajpai, 2023). While this book presents distilled insights in an accessible format, the thesis offers the theoretical scaffolding, data depth, and methodological choices that shaped the findings. Grounded in a constructivist grounded theory (CGT) approach, my research sits firmly within a social constructivist paradigm. Thus recognising that meaning is not some universal truth waiting to be discovered but constructed; both by executive coaches who were my respondents and by me as the researching practitioner through an active relational interaction of a semi-structured interview. The methodological choice of CGT was driven by the fact that I wasn't looking to test a hypothesis or predict outcomes. Instead, I sought to understand a live, evolving phenomenon from the inside out—*how executive coaches were experiencing digitalisation, in their own words, contexts, and reflections.*

To do this, I conducted semi-structured interviews with 25 experienced executive coaches. These recorded interviews were then transcribed and coded line by line. Using a process of iterative coding and parallel memo-writing allowed insights to emerge inductively from the data. The respondent group (detailed profile in the Appendix) was diverse in both geography and experience: participants were based across Europe, Asia, Africa, and North America, with coaching experience ranging from 7 to over 25 years. Most had worked extensively with senior leaders in multinational contexts and were familiar with both in-person and virtual coaching formats. Viewed together, this was a cohort of highly experienced professionals, each with a well-established coaching practice and an average of over a decade of experience,making them particularly well-positioned to explore the topic both broadly and in depth.

The interviews, analysis, and theory-building followed a multi-phased, rigorous process of open, focused, and theoretical coding, adhering to the grounded theory tradition (Charmaz, 2014). The methodology chapter of the thesis provides reflections on the ontological and epistemological underpinnings, along with respondent recruitment, ethical considerations, quality criteria, and the reflexive stance I maintained throughout. For those interested in exploring how digitalisation is shaping the field not just practically but epistemologically, the thesis serves as both a map and a mirror, mapping emergent themes while mirroring the researcher's own positioning and learning. Together with the 4-Winged Framework© and Coaching Continuum Framework© introduced later in this book, it offers a theoretical and practical toolkit for those who want to extend this conversation in research, training, or supervision contexts.

Data Collection During COVID-19

When I began my research journey in 2018, I had no idea that most of my data would be collected during a global pandemic. While a few initial interviews were conducted before March 2020, the bulk of my conversations with executive coaches unfolded right in the middle of the global crisis of COVID-19 (WHO, 2020). That timing changed many things. It shifted not just the *how* of the research,but also the *why* and *what.*

What had begun as a study exploring digitalisation's impact on executive coaching quickly found itself situated in a world where virtual interactions had become the norm, not by design, but by necessity, and not only for coaches but anyone across the world wanting to connect. As the world went into lockdown and everything moved online, coaching had to adapt. Coaches who had spent years working face-to-face were suddenly coaching entirely through screens. Naturally, the topic of virtual coaching, which had initially appeared as one of several important strands, moved to the foreground, and the fact that my interviews were now conducted over Zoom further underlined the subject.

As lockdowns became routine and physical offices disappeared from view, the very nature of coaching practice began to shift. The respondents I spoke with weren't simply reflecting on their coaching experiences from a distance, they were immersed in change, navigating both professional and personal disruption. Emotional strain, societal anxiety, and deep fatigue were no longer theoretical, they were present in the (*virtual*) room. While my research had set out to explore how digital forces were reshaping coaching, the pandemic illuminated just how deeply context shapes our conversations, our presence, and our sense of connection.

The COVID-19 crisis, therefore, didn't just influence the *method and data collection* of my research, it also shaped its *heart*. It brought digitalisation and virtual sessions into sharp focus and made the questions feel immediate and personal. Coaches weren't just talking about forces of change; they were living them, adapting to them, sometimes resisting them, and often making sense of them as we spoke. I share this context because it matters. It shaped the tone, the stories, and the reflections in this book. I share this background not merely to document the setting in which this research occurred, but to offer a simple reminder: context matters. As with coaching itself, research is shaped not only by what we explore, but by *when* and *where* we explore it. And often, what we see depends entirely on where we stand.

We don't see things as they are, we see them as we are.

Anaïs Nin (1961)

References

Bajpai, B. (2023). *Coaching in the digital age: How is digitalisation influencing executive coaching? A grounded theory exploration*. Oxford Brookes University.

Carroll, L. (1992). *Alice in Wonderland*. Wordsworth Editions.

Charmaz, K. (2014). *Constructing grounded theory*. Sage.

Nin, A. (1961). *Seduction of the Minotaur*. Swallow Press.

WHO. (2020). WHO Director-General's opening remarks at the media briefing on COVID-19—11 March 2020. www.who.int/dg/speeches/detail/who-director-general-s-opening-remarks-at-the-media-briefing-on-covid-19---11-march-2020.

Introduction

Why This Book?

Chances are, you woke up this morning to the sound of an alarm, not from a clock on your bedside table, but from a phone beside your pillow. Before you even stepped out of bed, you might have checked your messages, scrolled through the news, glanced at your email, or dipped briefly into a social media feed. Perhaps a few of you even started your day with a mindfulness app or a quick guided workout, while your smartwatch quietly logged every heartbeat, calorie, and step. As I write this sentence, I'm doing what most writers do every day. Typing on my laptop, switching between multiple screens, toggling between tabs of internet research and older drafts, all the while trying to resist the notifications that might pop up on my other devices, to stay focused on these sentences.

This digital pulse has become so woven into our days that we barely notice it. It's invisible and constant, like a constant hum or background music you don't even remember turning on. For example, it is highly likely that most of you reading this passage are using an electronic medium—a laptop, tablet or a mobile screen, without even realising how recent these changes are within the arch of the long human history.

You may be wondering why I'm beginning a book on coaching with such a description of the morning routine, digital hum, and connected devices. Some of you may even critically observe why the other morning activities like brushing teeth, making tea, or getting dressed find no mention?

Here's the thing: those daily acts, bathing, brewing, brushing, haven't changed much in the last 50 or maybe even 100 years, but our interaction with the world has. And that shift has come, quietly but completely, through forces of digitalisation. And yes, I am aware of the omissions I make of electronic brushes, smart showers, and Wi-Fi-enabled kettles, but I am sure if you reread the previous two sentences, you will still agree.

DOI: 10.4324/9781003638834-1

Even if your kettle or your toothbrush isn't yet connected to the cloud, chances are your life is. Whether it's health tracking, content consumption, or relationship management, most of us now move through our days accompanied by digital co-pilots. Each of us has a slightly different list of devices, platforms, and apps, but the point is the same: technology is not a layer anymore, it's the water we swim in. A quote by Levine and Dean (2013), "It's only technology if it happens after you were born", helps us understand why what feels like a disruption to one generation is a default for the next. Digitalisation is not just about tools or devices, it's about the shift in how we live, work, learn, relate, and lead.

What's true for our mornings and personal lives is even more visible across organisations. I am confident most of you have experienced the impact of increasing digitalisation in the organisations you work for or interact with. These organisations could be in health services (through telemedicine), retail (through click-and-collect), delivery (through Amazon same day delivery), academic institutions (through e-learning and MOOCs), large multinationals (through video conferencing and CRM transformations), small and medium enterprise (through ERP solutions), government (through e-governance), or even a solo entrepreneur (through digital marketing). No organisation is immune to the forces of digitalisation, and the examples shared are just a small sample to illustrate the scope of change, digitalisation is reconfiguring the very fabric of work.

Scholars Brennen and Kreiss (2016) define digitalisation as "the sweeping force of change arising from increased use of digital and computer technologies". While more discussion on this follows in later chapters, this succinct and well-crafted definition remains the working one for digitalisation through this book. I find the words *sweeping*, *increased*, and *force* incredibly apt. This is not a minor adjustment, it's a tectonic shift.

Which brings us to the question at the heart of this book.

If digitalisation is transforming how we live and lead, it must also be transforming how we **coach**, and how our clients experience **coaching**. The forces of digitalisation are for sure reshaping coaching relationships, redefining presence, and challenging the very notion of depth. They introduce new possibilities and new vulnerabilities through AI, data, and digital platforms. In doing so, they are changing not just *how* we coach, but also *why*, *where*, and *for whom* we do it.

This book is born from that realisation, from a growing awareness that the coaching profession, which at its core is about maximising human potential and could be a potent force for social change, rooted in presence, trust, and human connection, is now being asked to adapt in ways it has never faced before. A practice once rooted in presence, trust, and deep human connection now finds itself navigating the unfamiliar terrain of digital mediation, virtual spaces, and artificial intelligence.

Even before I formally began my doctoral research, which then led to this book, the seeds of this exploration were already present, in conversations, observations, and offhand remarks that lingered long after. I remember one such moment during a casual catch-up with a few coach friends. We were talking about how each of us was experiencing the effects of digitalisation in our coaching practice. One of them, a film-loving executive coach, put it rather memorably. She said, "For me, this shift feels like going from watching the special effects in a spaghetti western of the 70s to watching Avatar in 3D for the first time". That metaphor stayed with me. Because like cinema, coaching too is being reshaped, not by changing its core intention, but by altering everything around it: the medium, the expectations, the pacing, and the tools.

The conversation also made me realise that I wasn't alone in grappling with these questions. Many coaches, especially those working with senior leaders in fast-changing industries, were beginning to feel the same undercurrent: digitalisation wasn't just changing *how* we coach, it was quietly reshaping *what* coaching is. And as with film, not all coaches have found the transition comfortable. Some are excited, others cautious, a few resistant. But very few are untouched.

Who Is This Book For?

This book, therefore, is written first and foremost for the **executive coach** who wants to skill up for this emerging landscape, someone keen to understand the impact of digitalisation on coaching, and who wants to stay informed through *research-based insights* into *virtual coaching* and its related challenges.

But it doesn't stop there.

If you are a **coach**, whether your practice focuses on *leadership*, *life*, *performance*, *business*, *teams*, *careers*, *relationships*, *parenting*, *purpose*, *spirituality*, or any other label you use, this book is for you, too. Because the forces reshaping executive coaching are not limited to the boardroom. They ripple across every domain where human development meets digital interface.

If you are a **leader** navigating the fast-moving terrain of digital change, or someone who supports, develops, or collaborates with leaders, you will find in these pages a practical lens to make sense of the shifting expectations around communication, presence, trust, and growth. This book is also written for **coach training institutes, universities offering coaching degrees**, and **coaching researchers**, to provide a grounded, practice-informed view of how digitalisation is reshaping the coaching field. And equally, for **buyers of coaching services**, from **HR leaders** to **talent heads, learning and development professionals**, and organisational sponsors, this book offers insight into what's changing, what to watch for, and how to make more informed, future-facing coaching decisions.

If you are still unsure, use the simple ten-question checklist at the end of this chapter, and if you answer five or more yeses, then you are likely to find this book useful. This book offers stories, research, tools, exercises, and questions, not to provide fixed answers, but to invite exploration. To help you and your clients not just respond to digital change, but lead through it.

The Question That Inspired This Book

As with most things in life, the origin roots (using a tree metaphor) of this book are spread widely across my life experiences, including conversations referencing Avatar 3D and Wi-Fi kettles. Within this vast network of roots, the ones closer to the trunk, a metaphor for the core ideas contained in this book, can be narrowed to my experiences as an executive coach over the last 15 years and a people leader across five countries in three continents over 30 years. Building the tree metaphor further and zooming in even closer, I can locate the source root or the origin story for this book to one specific coaching incident around the end of 2017. We were living in London, and I, having completed my coaching diploma from Cambridge the year before, was taking on more executive coaching clients. It is in this background that the idea for my doctoral thesis, which then eventually led to this book, surfaced, unexpectedly, at the end of a routine coaching session.

My Alexa Moment: Origin Story

It had been an intense hour of coaching with a 51-year-old CXO from the Czech Republic, whom I will refer to as Petra.[1] Petra is an accomplished and respected leader in enterprise technology. We were meeting virtually, and while our physical distance spanned continents, the emotional connection had been strong during the coaching session. During this particular session, Petra was unsettled, visibly anxious. Something at work was shifting beneath her feet, and as happens often, the resulting instability had seeped into our coaching conversation.

As we explored, patterns began to emerge. What Petra described was not just the usual challenges of the workplace. It was something bigger, more existential—a creeping uncertainty about the new rules of work, communication, and relevance in her organisation. "It feels like we're living through a series of tragedies[2] emerging from digital disruptions", she said. We both smiled at the Greek reference, but the naming of "tragedies" helped, as our conversation flowed more freely, and insights surfaced. And Petra left with greater clarity, a few strategies to experiment with, and a lot to reflect on.

But the moment that stayed with me came just as she was logging off. With a half-laugh and a hint of seriousness, Petra said, "If this continues, it will not surprise me if I will be coached by an Alexa soon". She chuckled again, then added, "Well, I wonder what will happen to all the executive coaches who will then have to compete with an Alexa".

I smiled in the moment, but the question lingered, and led me to eventually explore the topic through a doctoral thesis (Bajpai, 2023). Now, as I write this book in 2025, we really don't have to wonder about Petra's remark anymore. Digital disruptions have only gathered further momentum over the last 8 years, and in just the last couple of years, large language models have gone from being academic curiosities to shaping daily conversations in boardrooms, classrooms, and coaching sessions alike. Technically speaking, today Alexa (or, for that matter, any AI system like ChatGPT, Claude, Gemini, DeepSeek, etc.) can simulate some aspects of executive coaching: *asking questions*, *tracking goals*, *offering reminders*, even *drawing from structured coaching models* to provide *feedback* or *suggestions*. But here's the crux, which many experienced coaches know intuitively: Executive coaching is not just about asking the right questions, it's about sensing the unsaid, navigating ambiguity, holding space, and adapting in real time to a client's emotional, relational, and contextual landscape.

What Petra had done in 2017 was to make me pause and ask: What happens to executive coaching in the age of Alexa? What becomes of presence when it is mediated by pixels? How is trust built across browser tabs? And what does learning mean when it is shaped by a machine? That exchange was the spark, the moment of clarity when I realised that coaching, like leadership and work itself, stood at a threshold. On one side lay the rich traditions of human connection, presence, and reflection; on the other, a tidal wave of digital change—fast, efficient, impersonal, and often unexamined.

This book is my attempt to sit at that threshold and make sense of what's coming. It draws from years of coaching experience, global conversations with fellow coaches, and my in-depth doctoral research of five years. But it all started, as all good coaching does, with a real conversation, a real person, and a question that refused to go away. Thank you, Petra!

Why Am *"I"* Writing This Book?

Like many things in life, this project is grounded in lived experience, personal, professional, and relational. This book draws heavily from two intertwined parts of my professional life: my three decades of experience as a people leader across industries and geographies, and my parallel journey as an executive coach over the last 15 years. These experiences didn't just shape my perspective, they shaped the questions I began to ask. And over time, those questions evolved into the inquiry that this book now explores.

Before I ever opened an academic journal on coaching, I had spent over 20 years navigating leadership roles across four industries, beverages, snacks, personal care, and telecom. That journey took me through many countries and cities, across functions like sales, marketing, digital transformation, and eventually into CEO-level responsibilities. Then, for the last 15 years, I was embedded in one of the world's largest telecom organisations, leading regional and global roles across 23 countries, both a participant and an observer of massive digitalisation-led change.

In parallel, during these same 15 years, I was also building my coaching practice. What started as an internal leadership initiative gradually evolved into a sustained executive coaching journey. Over time, I worked with over 500 clients in more than 15 countries, across sectors and cultures, some engagements formal, others pro-bono, many deeply personal. About half of that work was with internal clients (within a Fortune Global-500 telecom organisation) at senior levels. The rest came from mentoring young professionals, students, and entrepreneurs, many of them navigating their own version of digital disruption.

It was during this coaching work that I began to notice a pattern: conversations were increasingly shaped by questions with digital fingerprints. Not just the obvious tools and platforms, but deeper currents, around identity, pace, presence, and pressure. At first, I chalked it up to VUCA (Bennett & Lemoine, 2014), the volatility, uncertainty, complexity, and ambiguity of today's world. But over time, it became clear: digitalisation wasn't just one more pressure on top of the pile, it was reshaping the pile itself.

And then came Petra's Alexa moment. That comment pulled the thread tighter. It sparked the realisation that these weren't just coaching topics, they were systemic signals of change. It made me ask: *What is coaching becoming in a digital world? And what must coaches become in return?*

Those questions eventually led me to Oxford Brookes and to a Doctorate in Coaching and Mentoring that began in July 2018. Many parts of this book draw directly from my doctoral research, which served as both a foundation and a springboard for the ideas explored here. Rather than presenting them in academic form, they have been repurposed, reworded, and restructured to speak more directly to coaches, leaders, and practitioners navigating the realities of a digitally evolving world. Readers who are familiar with my thesis will recognise several passages, concepts, and references, this is by design, not oversight. The intention has never been to conceal the origin of these ideas, but to give them a more accessible, practice-oriented voice while staying true to their research roots.

But the book you hold in your hands, while enriched by my research, didn't begin in a classroom or a library. It began, as most meaningful things do, in practice, in conversation, and in the quiet persistence of curiosity.

How to Use This Book?

For ease of reading and reflection, this book is structured into four parts.

Part 1 titled "Understanding a Digitally Transforming World" begins with this introduction, followed by two chapters that set the stage by exploring the digital world we now live in, and how digitalisation is reshaping organisations, cultures, leadership expectations, and, as a result, the coaching ecosystem itself.

Part 2 titled "The Changing Experience of Coaching" presents the heart of my doctoral research and findings. It contains four chapters. They delve into the key themes that emerged: how coaches are experiencing change, how presence is evolving in virtual settings, how new opportunities are emerging and how coaches are reacting to the rise of AI tools and digital platforms.

Part 3 titled "Reimagining Coaching for a Digital Future" looks forward. Chapter 7 draws the threads together and introduces the **4-Winged Framework©**, a model for navigating this new coaching landscape. The next chapter offers a practical roadmap for coaches and leaders by introducing the **Coaching Continuum Framework©**. This section discusses the ramifications of a new vocabulary and gets into specific topics, including the idea of radical empathy, that are critical for the coaching industry in Chapter 9.

The final section, **Part 4** titled "Reflections and Continuing Conversations", contains a brief discussion on contribution to theory and practice, and details of my research participants. This section concludes with some personal reflections and discussion of the limitations and contributions of this book.

You're welcome to read the book in any order that suits your interests. That said, I recommend following the chapter sequence within each part to fully appreciate the build-up of ideas—especially in Part 1 and Part 3. The findings in Part 2 can be read non-sequentially, though I suggest reaching Chapter 6 only after going through the three that precede it.

Many chapters include reflective prompts and exercises. Use them. Mark the margins. Question what you read. Coaching thrives on relationality and active engagement, and so does this book. That's why I've subtitled it *A Practical Guide*. I hope you find it both practical and useful in your journey.

> Technology is nothing. What's important is that you have a faith in people, that they're basically good and smart, and if you give them tools, they'll do wonderful things with them.
>
> (Steve Jobs, June 13, 1983)

Reflective Exercise I.1 Is This Book for You? Ten Question Checklist

If you're still wondering whether this book is for you, take a moment with the questions below.

If you answer "yes" to five or more, chances are you'll find real value in the pages that follow, through stories, research, tools, and reflection prompts designed for your context.

1. Do you work in a helping or developmental profession where your conversations with clients often happen over video calls (Zoom, Teams, Meet, etc.)?
2. Have you ever wondered how digitalisation is changing the expectations placed on leaders, and how coaching should evolve in response?
3. Have you ever felt more exhausted after a day full of virtual meetings than after a full day of in-person sessions?
4. Do you sometimes struggle to build the same level of connection or presence in virtual coaching sessions as you do face-to-face?
5. Are you involved in shaping, delivering, or participating in coaching or leadership programs moving towards hybrid or digital formats?
6. Do you feel the need to stay current with the latest coaching research, especially around technology, virtual presence, and digital delivery?
7. Does your work depend on or regularly involve digital tools, platforms, or data systems?
8. Are you curious, or concerned, about the rise of AI-powered coaching tools, bots, or digital platforms in your profession?
9. Have you ever had to choose between travelling long distances for a coaching session and compromising by going virtual, even when it didn't feel ideal?
10. Do you believe that coaching can be a force for positive change, not just for individuals, but for organisations and society, and are looking for ways to adapt it meaningfully to today's world?

Five or **more yeses?**

This book is written with you in mind. Let's explore together how **coaching** can stay human, relevant, and impactful—**in the age of digitalisation**.

Notes

1. All mentions of real clients and people in this book are anonymised to protect confidentiality.
2. While quoting participants in this book, I have chosen to retain their original spoken words as they were expressed during our conversations. The style may feel informal and/or include grammatical slips. This has been done to preserve the authenticity of voice and expression. Clarifying words added by me appear in [brackets].

References

Bajpai, B. (2023). *Coaching in the digital age: How is digitalisation influencing executive coaching? A grounded theory exploration.* Oxford Brookes University.

Bennett, N., & Lemoine, J. (2014). What VUCA really means for you. *Harvard Business Review*, *92*(1/2). https://ssrn.com/abstract=2389563.

Brennen, S., & Kreiss, D. (2016). Digitalization. *The international encyclopedia of communication theory and philosophy*. https://onlinelibrary.wiley.com/doi/abs/10.1002/9781118766804.wbiect111.

Jobs, S. (1983, June 13). *Speech to International Design Conference [transcript]*. The Steve Jobs Archive. https://book.stevejobsarchive.com.

Levine, A., & Dean, D. R. (2013). It's only technology if it happens after you are born. *Journal of College Admission*, *220*, 6–12.

Part 1

Understanding a Digitally Transforming World

1 The World We Live In

1.1 Defining the Ground We Stand On

Before we start, it would be helpful to have a shared understanding of a few key terms, otherwise, we risk walking in different directions while thinking we're on the same path. This chapter is constructed using a nested framework©, which will be introduced through Figure 1.1—starting wide with the digital world we now live in, narrowing to the impact on organisations, and then zooming in on what this means for executive coaches and coaching. But before we step into that framework, two terms need to be properly defined: *digitalisation* and *executive coaching*.

Both may seem familiar, almost too familiar. But as with many things we take for granted, it's easy to have differing interpretations without being aware of them. Rather than assuming a common meaning, I offer the working definitions I've used in this book. These aren't the only definitions out there, but they provide the ground we'll be standing on as we go forward in this book. You'll find a reflective prompt at the end of this chapter that invites you to engage more deeply with these definitions and question what they mean in your own context. But for now, I'd encourage you to simply hold them as working anchors, definitions that don't limit, but orient. Because definitions matter, not to box us in, but to make sure we're starting from the same place before we explore what lies ahead.

Digitalisation

Let's begin with *digitalisation*, a word we're all familiar with, and yet, it can mean different things. The Cambridge Dictionary (2022) gives a straightforward explanation of the word "digitalise" as "to

DOI: 10.4324/9781003638834-3

change something such as a document to a digital form (= a form that can be stored and read by computers)". While technically accurate, this definition feels like we are still living in the days of scanners and floppy disks. It reflects a very narrow view of digitising, maybe accurate, but not quite what we're dealing with anymore. Such narrow references were the norm until the start of the century. Today, digitalisation is about how the widespread use of digital technologies is reshaping our lives, our work, and our relationships with each other. It's no longer just about tools, it's about a shift in the way we live, think, connect, and make decisions and its pervasive nature in transforming and influencing our world (Stolterman & Fors, 2004).

The definition that I found particularly appropriate comes from scholars Brennen and Kreiss (2016, 2019), who describe digitalisation as the *sweeping forces of change* driven by digital and computer technologies. I find that phrase, *sweeping forces of change*, both apt and powerful. Because that's what it feels like. Not a gentle update or an optional add-on, but a deep and ongoing transformation that cuts across industries, cultures, and ways of being.

In this book, I work with a definition that builds on this idea and adds the impact of the forces of digitalisation in the form of the Fourth Industrial Revolution (Schwab, 2016). Thus, digitalisation in this book is defined as:

> ***The forces of change arising out of widespread use of digital and computer technology, which are transforming the organizations, society and world at large, leading to the Fourth Industrial Revolution.***

This definition doesn't limit the conversation, it just sharpens the lens. Because digitalisation isn't just background noise in coaching today; it's quietly reshaping the room itself, even when it goes unnamed.

Executive Coaching

Executive coaching is a young field, just about four decades old, but in that short span, it has grown into a multi-billion-dollar global profession. The report by the International Coaching Federation (ICF, 2023) estimated there are over 100,000 professional coaches worldwide, contributing to a $4.5 billion industry.

Much like the world it serves, executive coaching has evolved with time. In the early days, it was often seen as a tool for fixing problematic behaviours in senior leaders. But as Coutu et al. (2009) noted, that view shifted. Today, coaching is more about developing high-potential performers and supporting leaders to grow, adapt, and lead in a complex, fast-changing environment.

Given how dynamic the field is, it's no surprise that scholars and practitioners have offered a variety of definitions. For those interested, I've included a meta-summary of these definitions at the end of this chapter as Table 1.2. But for this book, and the research that underpins it, I've worked with an adapted definition that draws from the work of Stokes and Jolly (2010, p. 244) and Cox et al. (2014, p. 2). The version you'll find here has been shaped to fit the context of this book and can be viewed through its parts emphasising *what it is*, *who's involved*, *how it's done*, *what it does*, and *for whom*. Thus, executive coaching for this book is defined as:

> ***A creative process of learning and leadership development, [what it is]***
>
> ***where a qualified coach external to the organisation works with the client, [who's involved]***
>
> ***through contracted and confidential one-to-one conversations, [how it is done]***
>
> ***to support desirable change and maximise the potential [what it does]***
>
> ***for the benefit of the client and potentially for other stakeholders [for whom].***

This definition sets the stage for what follows. At its core, coaching is built on the belief that people can grow, shift, and find new ways of living and leading, not only through instruction, but through joint exploration, reflection, challenge and support. As the rest of this book will show, the forces of digitalisation are now shaping that very process in powerful, sometimes unexpected ways.

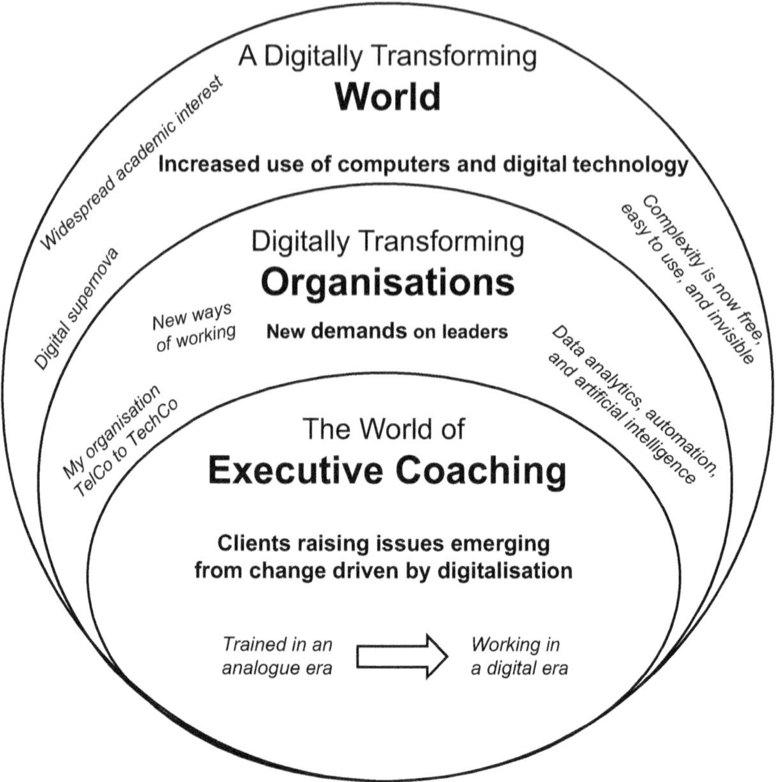

Figure 1.1 The Nested Framework©

1.2 A Digitally Transforming World

Most of us don't need a book to tell us that the world around us is changing. We feel it in our fingertips, in our workflows, in our everyday routines. The earlier example of our morning routines, starting with scrolls on our digital devices and ending with smart toothbrushes, wasn't just a storytelling device. It reflected how deeply digitalisation has woven itself into the fabric of daily life. Thomas Friedman (2017) calls this shift a "*digital supernova*"—a term that captures the sheer scale, speed, and unpredictability of what's unfolding. It's not one big change. It's a constant wave of changes. And what's fuelling it is an increasingly pervasive digital infrastructure, spanning homes, organisations, cities, and entire nations. We're no longer talking just about computers and mobile phones. We're now seeing smart sensors, learning algorithms, and digital systems that can perform tasks which, not long ago, needed human judgment (Bailey et al., 2022). These aren't isolated innovations. They're part of a wider transformation that's altering how we live, work, learn, and lead (Baptista et al., 2020).

Naturally, this has sparked academic curiosity. Researchers have begun exploring the human–tech interface across all kinds of domains, from *human resource management* (Votto et al., 2021) to *education* (Benavides et al., 2020), from *psychology* (Ostermann et al., 2021) to *psychotherapy* (Simpson et al., 2021), just to name a few. We are seeing entire professions reimagine themselves in response to digital possibilities. And with the COVID-19 pandemic accelerating the digitalisation agenda, this academic interest intensified almost overnight.

Which brings me to a challenge I face in writing this section.

How does one describe something as vast and evolving as a digitally transforming world—without oversimplifying it, or writing another book altogether?[1] If I try to include everything, this chapter would go in a thousand directions. If I trim it down too much, it would lose weight. So, I chose a middle path: to offer a brief history of digitalisation, summarised in Table 1.1. Adapted from the works of Heslop (2019) and Press (2015), it traces the broad arc of digitalisation, capturing key milestones and shifts that help readers see its evolution clearly, without getting lost in unnecessary detail. I do this to avoid the challenge of either being too narrow or getting lost in the scale. I have also included a reflective exercise at the end of this chapter, which invites you to interact with this table, not just to absorb it, but to consider: *What does a digitally transforming world look like in your context? And how has it shaped the way you live, lead, or coach?*

To make sense of digitalisation through Table 1.1, it helps to look at a few key turning points in the journey. Until 2007, the pace of change was fast, but largely tied to specific technological leaps. Then came what Friedman (2017, p. 22) called a watershed year: "the platforms birthed around the year 2007 surely constituted one of the greatest leaps forward in history". These platforms have since evolved to operating systems (Microsoft Windows and Linux), Apple's offerings (iPod, iPhone, iPad, iOS, iTunes, App Store), Google's search engine and Android OS for phones. They have led to the birth of social networking sites such as Facebook, LinkedIn, Instagram, and X (formerly Twitter). Also, 2007 marks the year when the process of digitising analogue and manual systems was pretty much completed across most organisations.

Table 1.1 A Brief History of Digitalisation

<table>
<tr><th>Year</th><th colspan="2">Key Milestones in the Digital Journey</th></tr>
<tr><td>1948</td><td colspan="2">Claude Shannon (1948), considered the father of modern digital communications, published “A Mathematical Theory of Communication”.</td></tr>
<tr><td>1956</td><td>IBM introduced the business world to magnetic disks and random-access data through the United Airlines reservation system.</td><td>1950s—Microchip and semiconductor transistors invented.</td></tr>
<tr><td>1965</td><td>Moore’s Law was published (1965). The constant doubling of transistors in an integrated circuit leads to years of doubling computing power and reducing costs.</td><td>1960s—First message sent over ARPANET, the foundation of the internet.</td></tr>
<tr><td>1971</td><td>Project Gutenberg was launched to provide copyright-free material electronically.</td><td>1970s—Home computers were introduced.</td></tr>
<tr><td>1982</td><td>The first commercial compact disc (CD) was produced.</td><td rowspan="2">1980s—World Wide Web invented; 8% of homes in the US have a personal computer.</td></tr>
<tr><td>1988</td><td>More CDs are sold than vinyl records.</td></tr>
<tr><td>1995</td><td>Toy Story, the first movie made entirely with CGI (computer-generated imagery), was released.</td><td>1990s—2G network introduced in Finland. Cell phones are sold commercially.</td></tr>
<tr><td>2001
2002</td><td>3G network launched in Japan
Digital storage surpasses non-digital storage.</td><td rowspan="2">2000s—Internet users reach a billion, and 50% of American households have a computer. 4G network launched (2009).</td></tr>
<tr><td>2007</td><td>94% of the world’s information storage is digital. iPhone, Hadoop, GitHub, Facebook (Sept 06), Twitter, Android, Kindle, and Airbnb launched.</td></tr>
<tr><td>2011</td><td>Amazon sells more Kindle e-books than print books.</td><td rowspan="4">2010 Onward—Digital Transformation. An organisation-wide change in people and processes driven by changing consumer expectations sweeps across industries.</td></tr>
<tr><td>2014</td><td>Worldwide, internet users reach 3 billion.</td></tr>
<tr><td>2016</td><td>The world’s first commercial virtual reality headset, Oculus Rift, was launched.</td></tr>
<tr><td>2019</td><td>5G networks launched.</td></tr>
<tr><td>2020</td><td>WHO declares COVID-19 a global pandemic.</td><td>Working from home becomes the norm.</td></tr>
</table>

Adapted from Heslop (2019) and Press (2015).

By the 2010s, the conversation had moved from digitising systems to transforming entire industries. In this phase, digitalisation was about reimagining work, communication, and leadership. Scholars called this the Fourth Industrial Revolution, also referred to as 4IR or Industry 4.0—an idea first proposed by Schwab (2016, pp. 1–2). He suggested 4IR to be a time marked by historic shifts in speed, scale, and impact, thus representing a significant shift in industrial capitalism. It is on this phase, roughly starting around 2010 onwards, the digital transformation era, that this book focuses. Consulting firm McKinsey (2022), referencing 4IR, suggests that the 21st-century industrial revolution is digital and refers to an "era of connectivity, advanced analytics, automation, and advanced-manufacturing technology that has been transforming global business". Figure 1.1 represents this transformation of global businesses, covered in the next section, nested within the outer ring of a digitally transforming world.

1.3 My Digitally Transforming Organisation

Writing about digitally transforming organisations (nested within the digitally transforming world) comes with the same challenge as the previous section, where to begin, and how to avoid getting lost in the scale of it all? The implications of the Fourth Industrial Revolution on Industry 4.0 are vast.[2] So instead of attempting a comprehensive overview, I've chosen to share something more personal: a short case study from my own organisation. While specific to my organisation, I hope this brief case study will illuminate the wider implications of the topic. The keyword for any good case study is "context", crucial to explaining the phenomenon (Yin, 2018), so that's where I start.

Between 2015 and 2020, I worked at the global headquarters of Vodafone in London, serving in a few global marketing roles. In 2015, Vodafone was a very large, very successful multinational in the telecommunications space. It had over 100,000 employees, operated across 26 countries, and had partners in an additional 55 countries. At the time, Vodafone was operating in a highly competitive and rapidly evolving telecommunications market, where both innovation and scale were critical to staying relevant. The rise of technologies such as big data, digital automation, and machine learning raised important questions about how the organisation needed to adapt. Under the leadership of CEO Vittorio Colao, Vodafone began a deliberate review of its ways of working to integrate these technological shifts. This organisational transformation journey is now well documented in a Harvard Business School case study by Kerr and Moloney (2019).

My years in Vodafone London (2015–2020) coincided with this significant wave of digital transformation across the organisation—impacting systems, structures, ways of working, and leadership experiences. In many of my internal coaching conversations during this period, executives raised topics directly linked to the ongoing changes. Vodafone had publicly stated its ambition to shift from being a traditional telecom company (TelCo) to becoming a technology company (TechCo). I began to notice that a significant portion of the coaching issues being raised could be traced back to the rapid changes driven by digitalisation.

Similar to my organisation, as more and more workplaces across the world become more digitised and e-working takes hold, core behaviours at work will begin to shift. Even long-standing organisational structures like hierarchies, reporting lines, and decision-making procedures get reconfigured. The rise of digital tools and the knowledge economy means that older systems built around command-and-control give way to roles that are more fluid, dynamic, and constantly evolving. In the next chapter, I'll use this foundation to focus on three specific areas of organisational change that are relevant for coaches and the coaching industry today. These are changing organisational structures, newer ways of working, and the evolving expectations placed on leaders.

Returning to my own organisation, this wave of digitalisation-driven change wasn't just operational, it was deeply psychological. Leaders were having to reconsider not only how they led, but also how they related to others, how they collaborated, and how they made sense of their evolving roles in a rapidly shifting environment. The impact of digital transformation wasn't something that stayed outside the coaching room; it entered with the client. You may recall Petra's case from the Introduction; her questions, her unease, and her reflection about being coached by an Alexa weren't isolated. They were part of a broader pattern I was seeing across my internal coaching sessions. The Harvard Business School case by Kerr and Moloney (2019) quotes the HR Director of Vodafone, highlighting the kind of shifts he expected from the leaders as part of this digital transformation: "[another] shift was moving from judgment-driven decision making to data- and AI-driven decision making. The final shift was a change in culture from a directive and hierarchical approach to one around empowerment, coaching, trusting people and holding them to account" (Ronald Schellekens, HR Director, Vodafone).

The Vodafone story outlines how digitalisation-driven change places new and often complex demands on leaders. This contains a requirement to shift their behaviours, which includes developing a more "coaching" style of leadership. And when the very nature of leadership begins to shift, it naturally raises questions about the role and readiness of those who support such changes—executive coaches. As we move to the innermost circle of Figure 1.1, the focus turns to what these shifts could mean for executive coaches and the coaching profession. As early as 2017, in my postgraduate paper, I wrote "executive coaching... probably also needs to evolve in the changing new digital-world of organisations" (Bajpai, 2017). That eight-year-old observation has only grown in relevance, and the final section of this chapter illustrates the same.

1.4 The World of Executive Coaching

History

"The coach began as a technology used for transportation, evolved into an object that was associated with a type of status and then becomes a prominent character in sport, before ultimately becoming an influential management concept". This tongue-in-cheek summary by Stec (2012, p. 331) captures the evolution of the word *coach*, while simultaneously highlighting a challenge the profession faces—its lack of a shared understanding.

While professional bodies like the ICF and EMCC have worked to bring structure through certifications and ethical standards, coaching remains an unregulated field, unlike psychotherapy or counselling. As a result, individuals who call themselves coaches often come from very different backgrounds and may mean very different things when offering their services. The spectrum is vast, ranging from the familiar domains of *sports coaching*, *life coaching*, *performance* and *academic coaching*, to the more esoteric *Akashic records coaching*, *tantric relationship coaching*, *alchemical performance coaching*, *chakra-alignment leadership coaching*, and *psychedelic integration coaching*. With such diversity, it's no surprise that clients sometimes find themselves confused, wondering what coaching really is, and whether it's right for them.

Thankfully, *executive coaching*, as defined earlier in this chapter, has developed a relatively distinct and consistent identity, particularly within corporate and leadership contexts. While some confusion still persists, the last three decades have seen executive coaching emerge as a more clearly defined practice, supported by growing academic literature and evolving professional standards (Bachkirova et al., 2016). While this book uses a strong definition (shared earlier in the chapter), it is also helpful to understand how other definitions of executive coaching have changed and developed over time. Table 1.2 offers a brief historical view of this evolution.

Table 1.2 Evolving Definitions of Executive Coaching

	Scholar	*Definition*	*Key Terms*
1.	**Levinson (1996, p. 115)**	"Executive coaching requires the ability on the part of the coach to differentiate coaching from psychotherapy, while using basic psychological skills and insights. It is usually short term and issue focused. At high executive levels, its success depends heavily on the consultant's knowledge about contemporary management and political issues".	– **Not** Psychotherapy – Uses **Psychological** Skills – **Short Term** – **Issue Focused** – For **Senior Executives**
2.	**Kilburgh (2000, p. 142)**	"A helping relationship formed between a client who has managerial authority and responsibility in an organisation and a consultant who uses a wide variety of behavioural techniques to achieve a mutually identified set of goals to improve his or her professional performance and personal satisfaction and consequently to improve the effectiveness of the client's organisation within a formally defined coaching agreement".	– Helping **Relationship** – By **External** Consultant – Uses **Behavioural** Techniques – **Goal Focused** – To Improve **Performance and** Personal **Satisfaction** – Helps **Organisation** – For **Managers**
3.	**Whitmore (2002, p. 9)**	"Coaching is unlocking a person's potential to maximise their own performance. It is helping them to learn rather than teaching them".	– Unlocking **Potential** – To **Maximise Performance** – **Learning** Focused
4.	**Bluckert (2006, p. 25)**	"The facilitation of learning and development with the purpose of improving performance and enhancing effective action, goal achievement and personal satisfaction. It invariably involves growth and change, whether that is in perspective, attitude or behaviour".	– Facilitating **Learning and Development** – To Improve **Performance** and Personal **Satisfaction** – Involves **Change and Growth**
5.	**De Haan (2011, p. 19)**	"Coaching is a method of work-related learning that relies primarily on one-to-one conversations".	– Work-Related **Learning** – One-to-One **Conversation**
6.	**Hawkins and Smith (2013, p. 28)**	Facilitation of performance improvement, adult learning, personal development/support, unlocking of personal potential and creative delivery of organisational goals.	– **Performance Improvement** – **Adult Learning** – Unlocking **Potential** – **Creative** Process

(Continued)

Table 1.2 Cont

	Scholar	*Definition*	*Key Terms*
7.	**Stokes and Jolly in Chapter 17 (Cox et al., 2014, p. 244)**	"For the work with senior level executives that focusses on the executive becoming more self-aware in order to carry out their leadership role more effectively… A form of personal learning and development consultation provided by someone external to the organisation who focuses on improving an individual's performance in the quintessentially executive role".	– **External** Coach – **Self-Awareness** Focused – Improving **Leadership** – **Learning and Development** Focused – **Performance Improvement**
8.	**EMCC (2018)** *Definition combines coaching and mentoring.*	"It is a professionally guided process that inspires clients to maximise their personal and professional potential. It is a structured, purposeful and transformational process, helping clients to see and test alternative ways for improvement of competence, decision making and enhancement of quality of life. Coach and Mentor and client work together in a partnering relationship on strictly confidential terms. In this relationship, clients are experts on the content & decision-making level; the coach & mentor is an expert in professionally guiding the process".	– **Maximise** Personal and Professional **Potential** – **Quality of Life** – Clients Are also **Experts**
9.	**ICF (2022)**	"ICF defines coaching as partnering with clients in a thought-provoking and creative process that inspires them to maximize their personal and professional potential".	– Thought Provoking – **Creative** Process – To **Maximise** Personal and Professional **Potential**

Missing Research

Table 1.2 reminds us that coaching is not a static practice, but a constantly *evolving* one. It's also a *relational* and *social process*, one shaped by the ongoing interaction between coach, client, and the wider organisational and societal context (Orenstein, 2002). Given that executive coaching works directly with leaders, within an organisational context, it would be reasonable to expect that a force as far-reaching as digitalisation, with its impact on social structures, organisations, and leaders, would be a major area of study in coaching research. But surprisingly, that isn't the case. The research remains limited, and this absence, given the scale and speed of change, is not just unfortunate, it's puzzling.

A meta-study by Athanasopoulou and Dopson (2018), based on a systematic review of executive coaching literature, strongly and probably for the first time in coaching literature makes an explicit acknowledgement that the socio-contextual impact has mostly been ignored in executive coaching research. The authors "argue that methodological rigor is as important as context-sensitivity" (Athanasopoulou & Dopson, 2018, p. 70)—a statement that should resonate with anyone working at the intersection of research and practice. Executive coaching, by its very nature, is shaped by and shapes the contexts in which it occurs (Giddens, 1984). Any serious exploration of executive coaching must consider the environment in which it is embedded. That has been one of the central intentions of this research: to bring the *context* into sharper view.

This chapter, through its nested framework©, paints a picture of that *context*, starting from the wider digital transformation of the world, narrowing into the organisational changes it drives, and only then arriving at its implications for coaching through its central research question—***How are executive coaches dealing with the impact of digitalisation?***

Gray et al. (2012, p. 124) ask two important questions in relation to change processes: "(a) What role does context play in shaping change? (b) Whose voice is being heard?" These questions apply directly to coaching. Executive coaching is, after all, a process designed to support change. And yet, much of the existing literature gives little space to the voice of the executive coach during times of systemic transformation. My research, and this book, aim to help shift that. It is this voice of executive coaches that governs and controls the narrative of this book, and I hope that you, the reader, many of whom will be coaches, find resonance and hear some echoes of your own story.

E-Coaching

The idea of remote or non-face-to-face coaching isn't new. Richard (1999, p. 28) was already discussing telephone and email-based coaching at the turn of the century, when he wrote "coaching can also include telephone sessions and even E-mail correspondence". Frazee (2008) was the first to use the term *e-coaching*, though her definition remained limited to *emails*, *texts*, *phone calls*, and *file sharing*, without any mention of video platforms.

The term *e-coaching* itself has evolved significantly over time. Initially used rather narrowly (and, arguably, incorrectly) to describe any remote coaching, it has gradually expanded to reflect technological shifts. Clutterbuck and Hussain (2010) widened the definition to include any learning dialogue supported by email or other media. Geissler et al. (2014) took this further, offering a more comprehensive view of e-coaching that included four specific modes: of "(1) audio communication (telephone), (2) video communication, (3) synchronous text-based communication, and (4) asynchronous text-based communication" (Geissler et al., 2014, p. 166).

It is helpful to identify e-coaching in this more comprehensive avatar. This helps distinguish e-coaching from remote coaching, which was essentially traditional face-to-face coaching supplemented by telephone, text, emails and sharing information electronically. As the mediums to connect have evolved along with digitalisation, an approach of locating the right medium for the right context and keeping in touch with the latest has only become more important. Kanatouri (2020, p. 15), in her book, provides a very good representation of the options available under the umbrella of e-coaching, which she has now termed as *digital coaching*. Kanatouri's framework maps digital coaching as a spectrum. It outlines three broad formats—**Remote, Blended**, and **Self-Coaching**—each varying in terms of how technology is integrated and who drives the process. Remote coaching can be led by a coach or done independently by the client, often supported by digital tools. Blended formats combine face-to-face sessions with either remote dialogue, digital tools, or elements of self-coaching. At its core lies the coaching dialogue, which may be supported, or not, by digital tools. The model reminds us that digital coaching isn't one thing, but many forms shaped by context, medium, and method.

The fact that 75% coaches were already using media other than face-to-face in the early 2010s makes it evident that *e-coaching*, in its evolved avatar of *digital-coaching*, has arrived and is here to stay (Boyce & Clutterbuck, 2010). In the backdrop of widespread adoption by organisations of video communication tools, it is probably not even a choice for executive coaches. To remain relevant in the digital age, executive coaches at the bare minimum need to be familiar and comfortable with the latest in video conferencing tools like Teams, Zoom, Google Meet, and Slack, to name a few.

So at one level, digitalisation is altering the tools we use; at another, it is also reshaping the environments we work in and the expectations placed on us. For executive coaches, understanding this wider landscape is not optional; it's essential. But before we turn our focus exclusively to the world of coaching, we need to step into the organisational layer more deliberately. The next chapter explores how digitalisation is transforming the structure of organisations, the ways people now work and collaborate, and the new kinds of demands being placed on leaders. These shifts form the backdrop against which coaching conversations unfold, and they deserve our close attention.

Reflective Exercise 1.1 Standing at the Threshold

Take a few minutes with the digital timeline in Table 1.1. Read it slowly, not just as history, but as a backdrop to your own story. Now reflect on the following questions—write in the margins, make notes, or simply pause and think:

1. What emotions come up when you think about how quickly digitalisation has progressed? Are you excited, curious, cautious, overwhelmed., or something else entirely?
2. Which milestone on this table feels most significant to you, and why? Does something stand out as a turning point in how you worked, lived, or related to others?
3. How has digitalisation changed the way you coach, lead, or learn today? Think about tools, platforms, rhythms, expectations, and how they've shifted.
4. If digitalisation were a colleague in your professional life, what kind of colleague would it be? Supportive partner? Demanding boss? Curious intern? Try giving it a character, see what emerges.
5. If you had to add one event from your own digital journey to this table, what would it be? Maybe it's the first time you used Zoom for coaching, adopted an AI tool, or ran a fully virtual leadership workshop.

Reflective Exercise 1.2 From Definition to Identity: What Does Coaching Mean to You?

Refer to the definition of executive coaching given in this chapter; note its five parts—(1) What it is "A creative process of learning and leadership development"; (2) Who are the Key Players "where a qualified coach external to the organisation works with the client"; (3) How is it done "through contracted and confidential one-to-one conversations"; (4) What it does "to support desirable change and maximise the potential"; and (5) For whom "for the benefit of the client and potentially for other stakeholders". Now evaluate and critique each of these five parts independently for your own coaching practice and create a definition for your own context and one you resonate with.

Reflective Exercise 1.3 Tracing the Digital Footprints of Change

Whether you're an internal coach within an organisation or an independent practitioner running your own coaching practice, digitalisation has likely touched your professional world in more ways than one. Take a moment to consider and make note of:

1. How has digitalisation changed the way your clients' organisations operate, structurally, culturally, or strategically?
2. What language do your clients (or your own business) use to describe this shift? Terms like *digital transformation*, *going agile*, *becoming a TechCo*, or *future of work*, what do they reveal about the underlying mindset?
3. Make a list of three meta changes which in your view are taking place in organisations you and your clients work in / work with.

Notes

1 For which I strongly recommend reading Friedman's book *Thank You for Being Late*, which over 486 pages does an excellent job of explaining our digitally transforming world.

2 To get a good understanding of those implications I recommend Klaus Schwab's (2016) book *The Fourth Industrial Revolution*, which outlines the forces impacting modern organisations. A trend fuelled by the fusing of physical, digital, and biological worlds and one he suggests will continue.

References

Athanasopoulou, A., & Dopson, S. (2018). A systematic review of executive coaching outcomes: Is it the journey or the destination that matters the most? *The Leadership Quarterly*, *29*(1), 70–88.

Bachkirova, T., Spence, G., & Drake, D. (2016). *The Sage handbook of coaching*. Sage.

Bailey, D. E., Faraj, S., Hinds, P. J., Leonardi, P. M., & Von Krogh, G. (2022). We are all theorists of technology now: A relational perspective on emerging technology and organizing. *Organization Science*, *33*(1), 1–18.

Bajpai, B. (2017). *How do authority figures influence, inform and impact my coaching practice?* Dissertation towards fulfilment of MSc in Executive Coaching, Ashridge (HULT).

Baptista, J., Stein, M.-K., Klein, S., Watson-Manheim, M. B., & Lee, J. (2020). Digital work and organisational transformation: Emergent digital/human work configurations in modern organisations. *The Journal of Strategic Information Systems*, *29*(2), 101618.

Benavides, L. M. C., Tamayo Arias, J. A., Arango Serna, M. D., Branch Bedoya, J. W., & Burgos, D. (2020). Digital transformation in higher education institutions: A systematic literature review. *Sensors*, *20*(11), 3291.

Bluckert, P. (2006). *Psychological dimensions of executive coaching*. McGraw-Hill Education.

Boyce, L. A., & Clutterbuck, D. (2010). E-coaching: Accept it, it's here, and it's evolving! In G. Hernez-Broome, L. A. Boyce, & A. I. Kraut (Eds.), *Advancing executive coaching: Setting the course for successful leadership coaching* (pp. 285–315). Wiley.

Brennen, S., & Kreiss, D. (2016). Digitalization. *The international encyclopedia of communication theory and philosophy*. https://onlinelibrary.wiley.com/doi/abs/10.1002/9781118766804.wbiect111.

Brennen, S., & Kreiss, D. (Producer). (2019, September 8). Digitalization and digitization. *Culture Digitally*. http://culturedigitally.org/2014/09/digitalization-and-digitization.

Cambridge Dictionary. (2022). Digitalize. *Cambridge Advanced Learner's Dictionary & Thesaurus*. https://dictionary.cambridge.org/dictionary/english/digitalize?q=digitalisation

Clutterbuck, D., & Hussain, Z. (2010). *Virtual coach, virtual mentor*. IAP.

Coutu, D., Kauffman, C., Charan, R., Peterson, D., Maccoby, M., & Scoular, P. (2009). What can coaches do for you? *Harvard Business Review*, *87*(1), 91–97.

Cox, E., Bachkirova, T., & Clutterbuck, D. (2014). *The complete handbook of coaching*. Sage Publications.

De Haan, E. (2011). *Relational coaching: Journeys towards mastering one-to-one learning*. John Wiley & Sons.

European Mentoring and Coaching Council (EMCC). (2018). *EMCC competence framework glossary (Version 2)*. EMCC.

Frazee, R. V. (2008). *E-coaching in organizations: A study of features, practices, and determinants of use*. University of San Diego.

Friedman, T. L. (2017). *Thank you for being late: An optimist's guide to thriving in the age of accelerations (Version 2.0, with a new afterword)*. Picador/Farrar Straus and Giroux.

Geissler, H., Hasenbein, M., Kanatouri, S., & Wegener, R. (2014). E-coaching: Conceptual and empirical findings of a virtual coaching programme. *International Journal of Evidence Based Coaching and Mentoring*, *12*(2), 165.

Giddens, A. (1984). *The constitution of society: Outline of the theory of structuration*. University of California Press.

Gray, B., Stensaker, I. G., & Jansen, K. J. (2012). Qualitative challenges for complexifying organizational change research: Context, voice, and time. *The Journal of Applied Behavioral Science*, *48*(2), 121–134.

Hawkins, P., & Smith, N. (2013). *Coaching, mentoring and organizational consultancy: Supervision, skills and development* (2nd ed.). Open University Press.

Heslop, B. (2019). A brief history of digital transformation. *The Network Effect*. https://supplychainbeyond.com/a-brief-history-of-digital-transformation.

International Coaching Federation. (2022). *ICF 2022 annual report* [Report]. coachingfederation.org

International Coaching Federation. (2023). *2023 ICF Global Coaching Study: Executive summary*. https://coachingfederation.org/wp-content/uploads/2023/04/2023ICFGlobalCoachingStudy_ExecutiveSummary.pdf

Kanatouri, S. (2020). *The digital coach*. Routledge.

Kerr, W. R., & Moloney, E. (2019). *Vodafone: Managing advanced technologies and artificial intelligence* (Harvard Business School Case No. 719-436). Harvard Business School Publishing.

Kilburgh, R. (2000). *Executive coaching*. Amercian Psychological Association.

Levinson, H. (1996). Executive coaching. *Consulting Psychology Review*, *48*(2), 115–123.

McKinsey. (2022). *What are Industry 4.0, the Fourth Industrial Revolution, and 4IR?* www.mckinsey.com/featured-insights/mckinsey-explainers/what-are-industry-4-0-the-fourth-industrial-revolution-and-4ir

Moore, G. (1965). Moore's law. *Electronics Magazine*, *38*(8), 114.

Orenstein, R. L. (2002). Executive coaching: It's not just about the executive. *The Journal of Applied Behavioral Science*, *38*(3), 355–374.

Ostermann, T., Röer, J. P., & Tomasik, M. J. (2021). Digitalization in psychology: A bit of challenge and a byte of success. *Patterns*, *2*(10), 100334.

Press, G. (2015). A very short history of digitization. *Forbes*. www.forbes.com/sites/gilpress/2015/12/27/a-very-short-history-of-digitization/?sh=1c9114e149ac

Richard, J. T. (1999). Multimodal therapy: A useful model for the executive coach. *Consulting Psychology Journal: Practice and Research*, *51*(1), 24.

Schwab, K. (2016). *The fourth industrial revolution*. World Economic Forum.

Shannon, C. E. (1948). A mathematical theory of communication. *The Bell System Technical Journal*, *27*(3), 379–423.

Simpson, S., Richardson, L., Pietrabissa, G., Castelnuovo, G., & Reid, C. (2021). Videotherapy and therapeutic alliance in the age of COVID-19. *Clinical Psychology & Psychotherapy*, *28*(2), 409–421.

Stec, D. (2012). The personification of an object and the emergence of coaching. *Journal of Management History*, *18*(3), 331–358.

Stokes, J., & Jolly, R. (2010). Executive and leadership coaching. In E. Cox, T. Bachkirova, & D. Clutterbuck (Eds.), *The complete handbook of coaching*. (pp. 245–256). Sage.

Stolterman, E., & Fors, A. C. (2004). Information technology and the good life. In B. Kaplan, D. P. Truex III, D. Wastell, A. T. Wood-Harper, & J. I. DeGross (Eds.), *Information systems research* (pp. 687–692). Springer.

Votto, A. M., Valecha, R., Najafirad, P., & Rao, H. R. (2021). Artificial intelligence in tactical human resource management: A systematic literature review. *International Journal of Information Management Data Insights*, *1*(2), 100047.

Whitmore, J. (2002). *Coaching for performance*. Nicholas Brealey Publishing.

Yin, R. K. (2018). *Case study research and applications: Design and methods* (6th ed.). Sage.

2 The Organisations of Today

2.1 Changes in Organisations

Given the scale and complexity of digitalisation's impact, it's not surprising that there is no single, cohesive view among scholars on how it is reshaping organisations. Instead, what we find is a wide range of interpretations, often overlapping, sometimes conflicting, on how digitalisation influences structures, learning, leadership, development, and coaching (Qiu & Pesch, 2019).

Kuusisto (2017) offers some clarity by naming a few key areas being impacted: organisational learning, structural design, agility, and the business ecosystem. Each of these carries significant implications, not just for systems, but for leadership and relationships within the organisation. Given empirical studies and robust data remain sparse, Alavi et al. (2014) propose a theoretically grounded hypothesis: that digitalisation leads to *flatter*, *more decentralised*, and *informal* organisations, characteristics that enhance an organisation's ability to respond swiftly to threats and opportunities, an ability essential in the digital age. At first glance, this trio—*flatter structures*, more *decentralised*, and *informal* organisations, may seem like abstract concepts best left to organisation design or HR specialists. But once we start paying attention, we see them shaping how decisions are made, how people interact, and how organisations are structured.

For instance, *flatter* organisations which reduce the number of hierarchical layers between the top and the front lines lead to senior leaders and CXOs routinely conducting open town halls, holding skip-level meetings or digital Q&As, thus directly interacting with team members who are many levels below in the formal hierarchy. It's not unusual to find a newly joined analyst participating in a Slack thread with a senior vice president, something that would have been unthinkable in an earlier, more layered structure.

DOI: 10.4324/9781003638834-4

Decentralisation is becoming more visible. Local teams are being empowered to make decisions closer to the customer, without always routing through central headquarters. Regions, countries, and even sub-national territories are beginning to play a more active role in strategic planning and design, moving beyond their earlier role as mere execution arms. This shift is partly driven by increasingly fragmented consumer needs, and partly by the fact that digital technologies now make it possible to respond to these micro-insights with speed and precision. A marketing team in Singapore might now launch a campaign in a matter of days, using live data, social media trends, and digital feedback loops, rather than waiting weeks for approvals from Europe or the US.

And *informality* is sneaking in, not necessarily in professionalism, but in tone and texture. Communication is now becoming more direct, less ceremonial. Emails have become shorter. Emojis appear in leadership posts. Senior leaders are recording short video updates rather than issuing long memos. The shift isn't about being casual, it's about being human in a fast-moving, digitally connected world.

Some researchers offer a different lens. BarNir et al. (2003) argue that it is not digitalisation that transforms structure, but rather the *age* and *size* of a firm that determines its digital readiness. In other words, older and larger organisations face more friction when attempting to embrace digital tools and the structural shifts they require. However, even within such firms, functions that are closer to the customer,like marketing or customer service, often find themselves at the frontlines of digital change. This may be due to direct pressure from digitally savvy customers, or simply the hard economics of cost-efficiency, something few CFOs will be willing to ignore.

Of course, we find critics who continue to question the causality of these trends. And they are right to remind us that organisations are shaped by multiple forces, not just digitalisation. But even with those caveats, patterns are beginning to emerge. The examples shared earlier aren't theoretical; they are drawn from everyday organisational life. And if they felt familiar, it's because they are already part of the fabric we're working with.

Digitalisation may not be the only driver of change, but it is undeniably one of the key forces enabling agility in enterprise 2.0, often through structures that are *flatter*, more *decentralised*, and more *adaptive* (McAfee, 2006). Today, much of the discussion in large organisations around organisation design elements like hierarchy, central control, and role flexibility is, directly or indirectly, shaped by the opportunities and pressures of a digital world. And these dynamics are no longer confined to large organisations alone.

In the social sector, NGOs and non-profits are also navigating the forces of digitalisation. While many operate with tight budgets and legacy systems, digital platforms have allowed them to reach new beneficiaries, manage distributed teams, and collect real-time data in ways that were previously out of reach, thus creating new designs, structures, and ways of working within these organisations. The adoption may be uneven, but the shift is irrefutable. From mobile-based health interventions to donor engagement on social media, digital tools are quietly reshaping how missions are delivered, measured, and sustained. While the next section of this chapter discusses these newer ways of working, the examples above are already making the social sector question the traditional structures they have been working with.

Start-ups, often heralded as digital-native organisations, seem like the natural winners in this shift. Many begin life *flat*, *decentralised*, and *informal*, by design. But as they grow, they often encounter the same tensions larger organisations face: how to scale without losing agility, how to formalise without becoming rigid, and how to build culture across virtual or hybrid teams. For founders and early leaders, digitalisation may offer speed, but it also raises questions about sustainability, cohesion, and leadership capacity.

Across all these contexts, whether in large organisations, start-ups, or NGOs, the influence of digitalisation on structure is real. It shows up in who makes decisions, how quickly things move, and what leadership looks and feels like. It changes how people relate to authority, to each other, and to the work itself. These structural shifts, don't exist in isolation. They influence how people actually work together, how decisions are made, how communication flows, and how collaboration takes shape. As structure changes, so too does the lived experience of work. And that's where we turn next: to explore how working, communicating, and collaborating are being redefined in the digital age.

2.2 Newer Ways of Working and Communicating

Leading Through Disconnection: Rajeev's Story (Case Study 1)

Rajeev, a senior leader in a global pharmaceutical company, had always led through relationships. He believed leadership lived not just in formal reviews or strategy decks, but in corridor conversations, quick check-ins, and the quiet cues people gave off when no one was watching. His team was spread across multiple cities, and he made it a point to travel regularly visiting teams in person, walking the floors, and hosting informal and formal dinners in the evenings. These rituals helped build more than alignment; they built connection, familiarity, and a shared rhythm of working together.

Then, suddenly, this rhythm got disrupted by COVID-19.

By mid-2020, Rajeev was leading entirely through screens. The pandemic had moved everything online, and with that shift came a new tempo. His calendar was now packed with back-to-back virtual meetings, with barely a pause to reflect, absorb, or connect between them. Conversations became tighter, more transactional, efficient, but stripped of the informal energy that once made his team feel alive. "I don't see them anymore", he told me in a coaching session. "I mean, I see their faces on a screen, but not the pauses, not the hesitation, not the energy in the room. I've lost the pulse, the little signals that used to tell me how people really are".

It wasn't about productivity. Rajeev said the work was getting done. But the way people worked, communicated, and collaborated had changed—subtly, but significantly. Some of the spontaneity was replaced by structure. Collaboration now looked like calendar invites. The human layer of leadership, the sensing, the adapting, the intuitive course-correcting, was harder to access.

Rajeev's story isn't an outlier. What struck me was not just his observations, but his discomfort with them. He couldn't quite name what was slipping away, but he could feel it. And he wasn't alone. I've heard versions of this story from many leaders and many coaches. Because when the structures change, the signals change. And when the signals change, how we work, how we communicate, and how we collaborate, all of it must evolve too. Even in 2025, with travel largely resumed and most pandemic-era restrictions lifted, the way organisations operate hasn't simply snapped back to 2019. The adoption of digital tools and the structural shifts they enabled have become embedded, altering rhythms, expectations, and norms. When I checked in with Rajeev earlier this year, his experience affirmed this: the landscape may have stabilised, but the way of working has irreversibly changed.

The ways we communicate and collaborate at work have been quietly but profoundly transformed by digital tools. What began as systems to support office tasks, emails, shared drives, messaging apps, have now become central to how people connect, organise, and build communities within the workplace (Baptista et al., 2020). These tools are no longer peripheral, they are part of the organisational fabric. Scholars like Dewett and Jones (2001) describe many of these digitally mediated "connections" as *weak ties*—the kind of interactions where people dip in and out, building surface familiarity rather than deep relational trust. Yet, as Rajeev's story illustrated, these weaker ties are not the exception but increasingly the norm for many teams, and they shape the tempo and texture of organisational life. Baptista et al. (2020) note that while digital workplace interactions are reshaping the modern organisation, this shift remains under-researched and poorly understood. What is clear, however, is that to function effectively, both organisations and their leaders must now engage fluently with digital communication and collaboration tools. These platforms affect more than just access to information, they subtly influence how familiarity is formed, how decisions are made, and how authority flows. The deep integration of these digital tools within the organisations now raises access, familiarity, structure, and power issues.

Some scholars have called for a rethinking of fundamental organisational practices, such as delegating, monitoring, cultivating relationships, and creating reflective spaces, precisely because these digital tools alter how those practices are experienced (Lyytinen et al., 2021). While most research still focuses on the behavioural use of these tools, a few have begun examining their deeper, organisation-wide impact (Baptista et al., 2010; Riemer et al., 2015). There are even early signs that these tools are gradually displacing more formal channels of influence, though such claims remain contested and under-evidenced. Baptista and colleagues caution us against romanticising these technologies. They remind us that digital tools, when deeply embedded, can create blind spots, narrowing how people interact and limiting the space for reflection. In their view, a more questioning stance is needed, rather than simply accepting these tools as neutral or inevitable.

What's emerging from the academic literature is a consistent thread: as organisations become flatter, more informal and decentralised, digital tools and technologies are becoming the connective tissue. They are the infrastructure through which information flows and coordination happens. When it comes to evaluating the impact of these digital tools and technologies, especially in human systems like coaching or learning, there's no single lens that fits. Much depends on how we choose to understand the relationship between the tool, the user, and the context in which both are embedded. Ertmer and Newby (2016) offer a useful framing by suggesting that technology and learning theory exist in a reciprocal relationship. Rather than treating technology as either a passive tool or an independent force, they propose a more dynamic view, where theory influences how tools are developed and used, and tools in turn reshape how theory evolves in practice. Their work draws on three major traditions in educational psychology: *behaviourism* (learning as response strengthening), *cognitive information processing* (learning as knowledge acquisition), and *constructivism* (learning as knowledge construction). In the first two, technology is often positioned as a means to *learn about* or *from* the tool. But in *constructivist* approaches, dominant in contemporary learning and coaching settings, the emphasis shifts. Here, learners are not just recipients, they are meaning-makers. And technology becomes something to *learn with*.

Borrowing from the learning sciences, particularly the constructivist uses of collaborative tools in Web 2.0 environments, we can see how these frameworks could inform the future of coaching research and practice. Sharples et al. (2005) add that learning no longer happens *in* a fixed context, but *with* it, through ongoing interaction between the learner and their environment. The context itself becomes fluid, shaped by mobile technologies, digital communication, and constant connectivity. This fluidity is not a threat, it's a call for responsiveness. As Bullen et al. (2011) and Creighton (2018) suggest, when collaborative tools enhance contextual learning, they don't just support knowledge transfer, they help build new ways of knowing.

As explored so far, digitalisation is not just altering organisations through flatter hierarchies, decentralised decisions, and more informal ways; it is also redefining the fabric of organisational life. Collaboration is now platform-driven, communication more fluid, and learning increasingly contextual. In this shifting landscape, leaders are not just adapting, they are being asked to embody change. The expectations placed on them now go way beyond strategy or delivery. It involves presence, agility, and the ability to lead when the rules are still being written. It is to these emerging demands on digital leaders that we now turn.

2.3 New Demands on Leaders

Most scholars agree (Avolio et al., 2014; Cortellazzo et al., 2019; Kane et al., 2019; Khan, 2016; Mohammad, 2009; Sheninger, 2019) that the emergence of new organisational forms and work environments led by digitalisation is creating new challenges for leaders and necessitates a leadership rethink. Yet, given the fragmented and interdisciplinary nature of leadership research across fields like management, psychology, and information systems, it remains difficult to extract a unified view. As Schwarzmüller et al. (2018, p. 14) point out, researchers continue to struggle "to detect larger patterns of change resulting from the digital transformation", including what it means for leaders of tomorrow.

Cortellazzo et al. (2019) attempt to bring some clarity by synthesising leadership studies across micro (individual) and macro (organisational) levels. Their analysis highlights two major shifts: first, that leaders are now expected to engage with a more *dispersed network of stakeholders* within decentralised systems; and second, that the ease of access to information demands leaders who can *facilitate collaboration*, often *across virtual boundaries and cultural divides.*

I recently coached a senior executive, Risha, who works for a global consumer goods company and was leading a regional initiative across South Asia. Unlike earlier models where strategy was "centrally crafted and locally executed", this time Risha was expected to engage a much *wider network of stakeholders*, from supply chain head in Vietnam to marketing lead in Sri Lanka to modern trade head in Thailand, all of whom had varying priorities, data, and market realities. Her challenge wasn't just alignment; it was influence without control, across functions and cultural contexts. Leadership in such settings is no longer about giving direction from the centre. It is about listening across layers and *networks of stakeholders*, *navigating complexity*, and building *shared ownership in systems* where control is distributed and relationships span beyond formal reporting lines.

At the same time, the ease and *speed of information* access have changed the expectations around how leaders show up. With real-time data, shared dashboards, and collaborative platforms now commonplace, teams often have access to the same information as their managers. The old industrial-era model of a leader who derived authority from having all the answers and controlled access to information is rapidly losing relevance. While experience earned through frontline problem-solving still carries weight, its shelf life is shrinking because the very frontlines where that expertise was gained have been fundamentally reshaped in the digital era. What worked earlier may no longer apply now, and relying solely on past playbooks is proving insufficient in today's fast-moving, networked environments. These shifts place less emphasis on the leader as the primary source of answers and more on their ability to *enable dialogue*, *facilitate collaboration*, and *hold space for ambiguity*.

These expectations have given rise to the concept of **e-leadership**—a term also explored by scholars (Avolio et al., 2014; Mohammad, 2009). While Goleman (2000) argues that core leadership competencies remain largely constant across both physical and digital contexts, others disagree. Mohammad (2009), for instance, proposes that virtual work settings fundamentally alter how leadership must be enacted, and calls for new models of leadership that recognise the shift from face-to-face interaction to digital interface. Avolio et al. (2000, p. 617) define e-leadership as "a social influence process mediated by advanced information technology to produce changes in attitudes, feelings, thinking, behaviour, and/or performance". Such reframing places leadership not in the individual, but in the dynamic interplay between *leader, technology*, and *context*. Lu et al. (2014) reinforce this view, arguing that leadership qualities cannot be transferred unchanged from analogue to digital settings, the context matters too much.

These discussions also suggest that digital technologies and leadership now exist in a reciprocal relationship. Leaders shape technology use, but they are also shaped by it. The context in which leadership takes place, distributed teams, screen-based interactions, informal collaboration, fundamentally alters what leadership looks like. This *social view of leadership* sees context not just as background, but as an active ingredient in how leadership is constructed and experienced (Avolio et al., 2014; Pulley & Sessa, 2001; Roman et al., 2019). This shift creates real and tangible challenges. Bell and Kozlowski (2002) point out that the two core functions of leadership, *performance management* and *team development*, can become harder to fulfil in digitally mediated environments. Distance, both spatial and emotional, dilutes traditional leadership cues. Leaders must now find new ways to create trust, convey intent, and develop people, often through platforms that were never designed with leadership in mind.

In response to these evolving demands, scholars have outlined a range of skills and competencies that leaders need to develop in the digital age, particularly to strengthen their capacity for **distributed** and **socially constructed** forms of leadership. Annunzio (2001) outlined seven such competencies; Kissler (2001) offered a different list of ten; and Avolio et al. (2014) emphasise the importance of balancing continuity with *adaptability*, *communicating purpose* clearly, and *leveraging digital tools to connect* with broader and more *diverse audiences*. However, as information becomes even more democratised and hierarchies increasingly fluid, these individual-centred models of leadership (Annunzio, 2001; Avolio et al., 2014; Kissler, 2001) may also need a rethink. Approaches such as *shared leadership* and *team-based influence* are gaining relevance, where leadership emerges from collaborative interactions rather than formal titles (Pearce et al., 2009). In such settings, leadership becomes a collective property, emerging from interactions rather than being assigned by title. These shifts, along with the growing acceptance of relational frameworks like *servant leadership* (Van Dierendonck, 2011), can be unsettling for traditional leaders accustomed to command-based authority and clear lines of control. This is precisely where executive coaches have a critical role to play, helping leaders navigate these massive shifts with clarity and confidence.

Leadership, or more appropriately, *leadership in the digital era*, is not only being redistributed, it is also being redefined. The boundaries are more porous, and the *power to influence* is increasingly shared *across networks*. Merchant (2012) suggests that in the social era, leadership power rests not with individuals, but with communities connected by digital platforms. This decentralisation extends even further in social movements, where scholars have observed the rise of horizontal leadership and digitally enabled group authority (Bennett & Segerberg, 2013). Leaders now face followers who are more autonomous, more connected, and more able to engage across layers of hierarchy. This places new emphasis on *two-way communication*, *influence without control*, and *fluency with digital tools*, not just for productivity, but for presence and connection.

Across leadership models, whether *competency-based*, *socially constructed*, *servant*, *shared* or *networked*, the message is clear: leaders must evolve. And as trusted thinking partners, executive coaches are increasingly being invited to walk alongside them in that evolution.

So, What's Next for Executive Coaches?

For executive coaches, these shifts are not peripheral context, they are becoming central to the coaching conversation. As leadership is redefined in more distributed, digital, and dynamic ways, coaching increasingly becomes the space where leaders pause to make sense of what that means for them. Think of Petra, who discovered new challenges for her leadership in a changing environment. Or Risha, who had to learn a new skill of managing distributed stakeholders. Or Rajeev, who struggled to lead without the informal signals he once relied on. In these conversations, leaders are beginning to explore unfamiliar questions, challenge long-held assumptions, and experiment with new ways of showing up in a world that no longer plays by the old rules.

The structural and behavioural shifts brought on by digitalisation don't stay in strategy decks, they walk into coaching sessions as quiet uncertainties: about presence, influence, and connection. Leaders may not always name these changes, but they feel them, in what's lost between video calls or missing from casual hallway chats. In this evolving landscape, coaches are no longer just helping refine behaviours; they are holding space for deeper transitions. Doing so calls for new sensitivities, the ability to notice the invisible weight of distributed work, the subtle reshaping of human presence through technology, and the shifting norms that now define what leadership looks and feels like.

This is where the next part of the book turns its gaze. The groundwork has been laid, the wider context explored, the organisational shifts mapped, and the emerging demands on leaders outlined. What follows now is an exploration of how executive coaching itself must evolve, what does it mean to coach in this digital age? What is changing in the coaching relationship, in the presence of the coach, in the topics clients are bringing and in the competencies required to be effective as an executive coach?

The chapters that follow explore these questions, not with prescriptions, but with reflections, research, and real-world experiences. Because executive coaching, much like leadership, is being reshaped not only from the outside in, but also from the inside out. And it's in that space, in the middle of complexity, ambiguity, change, evolution, and human connection, that the coach's role becomes not just relevant, but essential.

Reflective Exercise 2.1 Spot the Shift

Take a moment to consider how the themes of *flatness*, *decentralisation*, and *informality* are manifesting in your own organisational or coaching context.

1. *Flatness*. Think about the last time you directly interacted with someone two or more levels above or below you (or your client). → *Jot down one example where hierarchy felt less important than connection*.
2. *Decentralisation*. Recall a decision made by a local team or individual without waiting for top-down approval. → *Describe a moment where someone stepped up—and didn't wait for permission*.
3. *Informality*. Look at recent communication, emails, updates, or meetings. → *Note an example of where a more human tone helped, or where its absence created distance*.

Now pause. Which of these shifts is most visible in your world right now? Which one feels most uncomfortable—or incomplete? → *Circle the one that most challenges your current assumptions about leadership, structure, or culture*. The idea is not to be diagnostic but to pay attention. Because what we notice is often the first step towards how we choose to respond.

Reflective Exercise 2.2 Reframing Leadership Questions

Take a moment to read a few leadership coaching questions listed below. In a digitally transformed world, some of these may need subtle, but meaningful, shifts. For instance:

- A question like "How are you managing your team?" might evolve into "How are you creating alignment across a distributed network?"
- "Where are you getting stuck?" could shift to "Where is clarity hard to find in your virtual or hybrid context?"
- And "What does success look like for your leadership?" might now invite a deeper reflection as "How has your definition of success shifted in a more fluid, digital world?"

Now try rewriting two of your own go-to questions, rephrasing them to reflect the new realities of digital leadership. Use them in your next session, and notice what opens up.

References

Alavi, S., Abd. Wahab, D., Muhamad, N., & Arbab Shirani, B. (2014). Organic structure and organisational learning as the main antecedents of workforce agility. *International Journal of Production Research*, *52*(21), 6273–6295.

Annunzio, S. (2001). *eLeadership: Proven techniques for creating an environment of speed and flexibility in the digital economy*. Simon and Schuster.

Avolio, B. J., Kahai, S., & Dodge, G. E. (2000). E-leadership: Implications for theory, research, and practice. *The Leadership Quarterly*, *11*(4), 615–668.

Avolio, B. J., Sosik, J. J., Kahai, S. S., & Baker, B. (2014). E-leadership: Re-examining transformations in leadership source and transmission. *The Leadership Quarterly*, *25*(1), 105–131.

Baptista, J., Newell, S., & Currie, W. (2010). Paradoxical effects of institutionalisation on the strategic awareness of technology in organisations. *The Journal of Strategic Information Systems*, *19*(3), 171–183.

Baptista, J., Stein, M.-K., Klein, S., Watson-Manheim, M. B., & Lee, J. (2020). Digital work and organisational transformation: Emergent digital/human work configurations in modern organisations. *The Journal of Strategic Information Systems*, *29*(2), 101618.

BarNir, A., Gallaugher, J. M., & Auger, P. (2003). Business process digitization, strategy, and the impact of firm age and size: The case of the magazine publishing industry. *Journal of Business Venturing*, *18*(6), 789–814.

Bell, B. S., & Kozlowski, S. W. (2002). A typology of virtual teams: Implications for effective leadership. *Group & Organization Management*, *27*(1), 14–49.

Bennett, W. L., & Segerberg, A. (2013). *The logic of connective action: Digital media and the personalization of contentious politics*. Cambridge University Press.

Bullen, M., Morgan, T., & Qayyum, A. (2011). Digital learners in higher education: Generation is not the issue. *Canadian Journal of Learning and Technology/La revue canadienne de l'apprentissage et de la technologie*, *37*(1). https://doi.org/10.21432/T2NC7B.

Cortellazzo, L., Bruni, E., & Zampieri, R. (2019). The role of leadership in a digitalized world: A review. *Frontiers in Psychology*, *10*, 1938.

Creighton, T. B. (2018). Digital natives, digital immigrants, digital learners: An international empirical integrative review of the literature. *Education Leadership Review*, *19*(1), 132–140.

Dewett, T., & Jones, G. R. (2001). The role of information technology in the organization: A review, model, and assessment. *Journal of Management*, *27*(3), 313–346.

Ertmer, P. A., & Newby, T. J. (2016). Learning theory and technology: A reciprocal relationship. In D. S. N. Rushby (Ed.), *The Wiley handbook of learning technology*. John Wiley & Sons.

Goleman, D. (2000). Leadership that gets results. *Harvard Business Review*, March–April. https://hbr.org/2000/03/leadership-that-gets-results.

Kane, G. C., Phillips, A. N., Copulsky, J., & Andrus, G. (2019). How digital leadership is (n't) different. *MIT Sloan Management Review*, *60*(3), 34–39.

Khan, S. (2016). *Leadership in the digital age: A study on the effects of digitalisation on top management leadership* (Master's thesis, Stockholm University).

Kissler, G. D. (2001). E-leadership. *Organizational Dynamics*, *30*(2), 121.

Kuusisto, M. (2017). Organizational effects of digitalization: A literature review. *International journal of organization theory and behavior*, *20*(3), 341–362.

Lu, L., Shen, C., & Williams, D. (2014). Friending your way up the ladder: Connecting massive multiplayer online game behaviors with offline leadership. *Computers in Human Behavior*, *35*, 54–60.

Lyytinen, K., Nickerson, J. V., & King, J. L. (2021). Metahuman systems= humans+ machines that learn. *Journal of Information Technology*, *36*(4), 427–445.

McAfee, A. (2006). Enterprise 2.0: The dawn of emergent collaboration. *Enterprise*, 2, 15–26.

Merchant, N. (2012). *11 rules for creating value in the social era*. Harvard Business Press.

Mohammad, K. (2009). E-Leadership: The emerging new leadership for the virtual organization. *Journal of Managerial Sciences*, *3*(1).

Pearce, C. L., Manz, C. C., & Sims, H. P. Jr (2009). Where do we go from here? Is shared leadership the key to team success? *Organizational Dynamics*, *38*(3), 234–238.

Pulley, M. L., & Sessa, V. I. (2001). E-leadership: tackling complex challenges. *Industrial and Commercial Training*, *33*(6), 225–230.

Qiu, Y., & Pesch, R. (2019). The impact of digitalisation on organisations: A review of the empirical literature. *Academy of Management Proceedings*, 2019(1), 16207.

Riemer, K., Stieglitz, S., & Meske, C. (2015). From top to bottom. *Business & Information Systems Engineering*, *57*(3), 197–212.

Roman, A. V., Van Wart, M., Wang, X., Liu, C., Kim, S., & McCarthy, A. (2019). Defining e-leadership as competence in ICT-mediated communications: An exploratory assessment. *Public Administration Review*, *79*(6), 853–866.

Schwarzmüller, T., Brosi, P., Duman, D., & Welpe, I. M. (2018). How does the digital transformation affect organizations? Key themes of change in work desin and leadership. *Management Revue*, *29*(2), 114–138.

Sharples, M., Taylor, J., & Vavoula, G. (2005). Towards a theory of mobile learning. In H. van der Merwe & T. Brown (Eds.), *Proceedings of mLearn 2005: 4th World Conference on Mobile Learning* (pp. 1–9).

Sheninger, E. (2019). *Digital leadership: Changing paradigms for changing times*. Corwin Press.

Van Dierendonck, D. (2011). Servant leadership: A review and synthesis. *Journal of Management*, *37*(4), 1228–1261.

Part 2

The Changing Experience of Coaching

3 Encountering Change

We have already set the scene. The **Introduction** and **Preface** pose the central questions and outline the scope of inquiry. **Chapters 1** and **2** map the context: the pace and scale of digital change, the changing organisational landscape, and the implications for leaders and for coaching practice. They also provide the working definitions, pandemic context, and conceptual frames you will need to read the empirical material that follows.

Part 2 shifts from context to evidence. It contains the heart of my research, where we shift from terrain to testimony. Over **four chapters**, I bring you the voices and lived experiences of executive coaches who were navigating this change in real time. We begin by exploring how coaches make sense of digitalisation, leading to greater need for empathy, then move to the felt losses of depth and presence, the new windows opened by virtual practice, and finally the complex feelings that AI and relevance provoke.

3.1 Digitalisation as Understood by Executive Coaches

Before diving into the core research question, **how were executive coaches dealing with the impact of digitalisation?**—it was essential to understand how the executive coaches made sense of the term *digitalisation* itself. After all, as with most things in life, what someone talks about depends heavily on what they think it means.

As a reader of this book, you already have the benefit of a shared working definition of digitalisation (covered in Chapter 1), along with a wide-ranging understanding of the context within which this phenomenon is unfolding, as well as its implications, all detailed in Part 1 of the book. However, my research participants came into the conversations without such shared frames. While they were aware of the

DOI: 10.4324/9781003638834-6

overall objective of my research, there was no formal priming or alignment on terminology or context before the interviews began. That wasn't an oversight, it was by design.

The foundation of my research was interpretive. One of the core assumptions of this stance is that people construct meaning through their lived experiences and social realities. My aim wasn't to arrive at a single, fixed articulation of the impact of digitalisation on executive coaching, but to explore how it was being understood and experienced by seasoned coaches in their own words and settings. To do that, I drew on interpretivist frameworks that allowed for multiple realities to emerge, recognising, as Holstein and Gubrium (2007, p. 345) put it, "the constellation of procedures, conditions, and resources through which reality is apprehended, understood, organized, and conveyed in everyday life".

This stance also positions the researcher not as a detached observer but as an active, reflexive participant. In this view, research is not a neutral mirror, it's more like a carefully stitched quilt, where each thread reflects both the voices of the participants and the perspective of the researcher. As Denzin (2009) suggests, no text is ever entirely free of its author's imprint. In a sense, the interpretations of the phenomena under study are as much the respondent's interpretation as those of the researcher.

Such an approach is particularly important when it comes to concepts like digitalisation. Each executive coach I interviewed brought their own understanding of the term, shaped by their unique context, experiences, and professional journeys. For some, it referred to specific tools or platforms. For others, it meant broader shifts in work culture, client expectations, or even identity. Their interpretations varied widely, and that variation was not just expected, it was welcomed. It aligned with the central tenet of interpretivism: that individuals encounter the same phenomenon from different vantage points and construct their own social realities accordingly (Saunders et al., 2019). However, my research was not merely an interpretive exercise in exploration and description, instead, it was a deliberate and purposeful process of meaning-making, aimed at elevating the data to a conceptual level. The goal was not just to understand, but to theorise, to generate insights that move beyond the immediate and towards a more structured understanding of how executive coaching is being reshaped by digitalisation, which are now presented in this book.

Diversity in meaning surfaced early in my interviews. One of my respondents, Paul, captured it succinctly when he said, "Because [digitalisation] it's such a broad term [thus, it is confusing]". That single remark reflected the complexity I was to encounter throughout the research, and set the stage for the first significant findings of my research.

Within the diverse understandings shared by my respondents, there was a general agreement that digitalisation will significantly impact the coaching industry. As Rohan, a seasoned executive coach, put it, "Is digitalisation going to have an impact on coaching? The answer is 100%", and all the other coaches interviewed agreed with the sentiment. What's more, there was a shared sense amongst the clients that the impact would not only be significant, but wide-ranging, touching nearly every aspect of how executive coaching is delivered, experienced, and valued.

By now, if you've made it this far in the book, and perhaps answered "yes" to more than five questions in the introductory checklist, this first finding may feel almost self-evident. Chances are, you not only agree with it but are also genuinely curious about what comes next. That same sense of agreement, and a deep interest in the topic, was also reflected in my research conversations. Every single participant engaged with focus, energy, and thoughtfulness during the interviews, underscoring just how present and real this topic felt for them. So, having established that the impact of digitalisation on executive coaching is both significant and far-reaching, let's not linger here. Instead, let's move forward to explore how these executive coaches actually understood, articulated, and experienced that impact in their own words and contexts.

As highlighted, during the research, it became evident that coaches were not working with a uniform understanding of digitalisation. Instead, they interpreted and experienced its impact through different lenses, each shaped by their own context, client work, and relationship with technology. While these interpretations varied, they broadly clustered into three distinct yet overlapping perspectives: one focused on *tools and technology*, another on *how coaching practice* itself *is being disrupted* particularly through *video-based coaching*, which had become especially salient during the pandemic, and a third adopted a broader approach, situating their reflections within the *wider context of digital life*, highlighting shifting organisational dynamics, evolving expectations of leadership, and the deeper societal transformation underway. Understanding these perspectives helps situate the responses and also provides a useful framework for reflecting on our own orientation to digitalisation.

1. **Tools and Technology in Focus:** This perspective frames digitalisation primarily as the integration of various tools that modify the logistics and delivery of coaching. Coaches who work from this lens often speak about technologies such as AI-powered scheduling assistants, encrypted cloud-based storage for client records, or digital goal-tracking dashboards. Their reflections tend to centre around platform preferences (e.g., Zoom vs. Teams), data security choices (e.g., cloud vs. local storage), or the comparative effectiveness of AI-generated coaching prompts (e.g., ChatGPT vs. Gemini). This view can be termed as a *functional lens*, where technology is seen as an enabler or constraint to the coaching process.
2. **Relationality Disrupted:** This perspective is rooted in the *felt disruptions* to coaching presence and relationship-building in virtual settings. Coaches viewing digitalisation through this lens often focus on the subtle yet significant shifts in how connection is experienced: the strain of back-to-back video sessions, the awkwardness of simulated eye contact through screens, or the layering of home-based distractions during coaching conversations. This *relational lens* places less emphasis on the technology itself and more on how it disturbs the interpersonal, embodied, and emotional quality of coaching. For these coaches, the shift to video isn't simply a technical adjustment, it's a relational recalibration.
3. **Coaching in a Changing World:** This perspective views digitalisation not as a set of tools or challenges, but as a *systemic transformation* that is redefining the landscape in which coaching takes place. Coaches adopting this lens spoke about working with leaders navigating hybrid team cultures, data-driven decision making, or existential fatigue from accelerated change. Here, coaching is situated in a larger narrative, one shaped by digital transformation, blurred work–life boundaries, and shifting organisational structures. This is a socio-contextual framing, which aligns with a constructivist paradigm, where meaning is co-created within a shifting environment. It was this systemic orientation that helped me identify the next significant finding in my research.

3.2 Direct vs. Indirect Impact

Building on the three lenses outlined earlier, the research revealed that a particularly useful way to deepen the *systemic* view is to distinguish between two interrelated types of impact: I termed them simply as *direct* and *indirect*. Without such a distinction, the systemic lens, though rich, can feel too broad, making it difficult to locate where and how digitalisation is actually showing up in practice.

The *direct impact* refers to changes in how coaching is being conducted. This includes shifts in the delivery medium (from in-person to virtual), the altered rhythms of sessions, and the increasing use of digital tools by coaches themselves. In essence, this is the impact on "how we are coaching". It aligns naturally with those working from the *functional and the relational* lens, where changes in tools and presence are front and centre.

The *indirect impact*, on the other hand, relates to how digitalisation is transforming the client's world. These are the changes that originate in the client's organisation, industry, or broader societal context. For example, this could relate to hybrid work cultures, digital decision-making systems, constant availability, or algorithmic performance reviews, much of it discussed in Chapters 1 and 2. These shifts shape the content and emotional tone of the coaching session, often surfacing as new anxieties, priorities, or identity questions. This is the "impact on our clients", and aligns with the *systemic* lens.

By separating the systemic view into these two dimensions—1) how coaching is changing and 2) how the client's world is changing, we gain a more structured and integrated understanding. It was also getting evidence that the three lenses (functional, relational, and systemic) are not neatly separated. Thus, a more helpful view would be to look at them as three overlapping circles of a classical Venn diagram. The demarcation of direct and indirect impact is a bit less overlapping and can help bring together all three interpretive lenses into a single, workable frame. This overlap of lenses and relatively larger separation of direct and indirect impact has been visualised in Figure 3.1. Here, the forces of digitalisation are positioned on the left and executive coaches encounter the resultant change next. This is followed by the three lenses and two dimensions discussed. Such a visualisation also reminds us

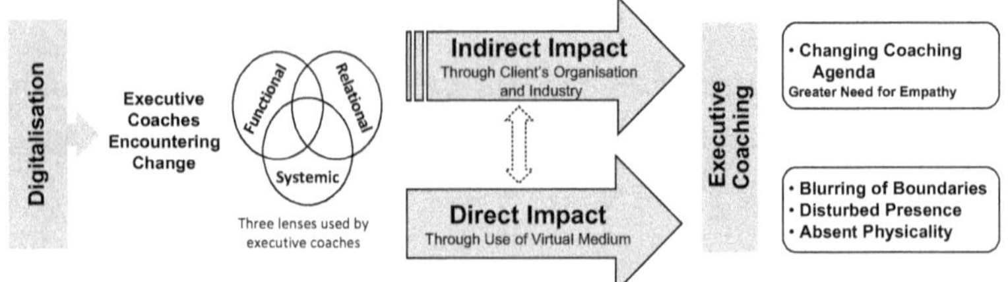

Figure 3.1 Direct and Indirect Impact

that digitalisation doesn't affect coaching from just one direction. It flows both ways as indicated by the dotted two-way arrow.

While simplistic at first glance, the framework of Figure 3.1 is helpful. A shared language, clear lexicon, or conceptual framework provides the grounding necessary to navigate the complex, multifaceted, and transformative socio-economic landscape of digitalisation. Without it, conversations can remain vague or superficial, lacking the clarity needed for meaningful engagement. Given the scarcity of research that meaningfully addresses the socio-contextual impact of digitalisation on coaching practice, this framework offers a much-needed starting point. It provides a foundation that researchers, practitioners, supervisors, and training or certification bodies can now engage with, critique, and build upon.

During my research, many coaches expressed frustration at the absence of any commonly accepted frameworks to articulate the impact of digitalisation, noting how difficult it is to engage with something "so significantly important, yet so poorly defined". The model introduced in Figure 3.1 aims to fill that gap by distinguishing between the direct and indirect impacts of digitalisation on executive coaching. It offers a conceptual anchor for ongoing research, informed dialogue, and deeper reflection.

One such deeper reflection, emerging from the indirect impact dimensions, led to the next significant finding of this research. As Chapter 2 highlighted, today's organisations are undergoing rapid transformation, thus placing new and often unfamiliar demands on leaders. As one coach noted, "Big changes... have got accelerated; distributed teams; distributed leadership; remote teams and how to manage these teams".

In response to these changes, many coaches expressed a growing sense that the executive coaching agenda itself must evolve to stay relevant. It is not enough to adapt tools or formats; the very substance of what is being explored in coaching conversations needs to shift. This realisation forms the basis for the next section, which explores how the coaching agenda is changing, and what that evolution might require from coaches.

3.3 Changing Evolving Coaching Agenda

Most of the respondents agreed that the executive coaching agenda must develop in response to organisational changes, and a few proposed an interesting framing of this relationship. Rather than viewing coaching as reacting to digital disruption, they suggested that coaching should actively enable and even lead organisational change. In their view, the question wasn't only *how digitalisation is impacting executive coaching*, but *how executive coaching can support and may lead organisations in navigating digitalisation-led changes*. Regardless of the direction of causality, there was universal agreement among respondents that the coaching agenda must evolve to remain relevant and impactful.

While scholars have located changing organisational structures (Alavi et al., 2014; McAfee, 2006; Riemer et al., 2015; Stray et al., 2020) and changing ways of working (Baptista et al., 2020; Dewett & Jones, 2001; Lyytinen et al., 2021) as key elements impacting organisations and leaders, my research surfaced a deeper, more foundational concern as pictured by executive coaches: *the increasing fragmentation of team interactions*. Driven by digital tools, virtual technologies, and asynchronous work patterns, this *fragmentation* emerged as an underlying force, something referenced in Rajeev's reflections in Case Study 1, and more prominently featured in Michael's story below.

Fragmented Teams, Newer Challenges: Michael's Story (Case Study 2)

Michael was coaching a CIO at a large German tech firm. Before the pandemic, his client had little interest in remote work. In his view, teams belonged in offices, anything else felt like a compromise. Then COVID-19 forced a change. Remote work became unavoidable. At first, the adjustment seemed purely logistical. The work continued, meetings moved online, and delivery remained reliable.

But something wasn't right. In coaching sessions, the CIO voiced an unease he couldn't quite name. He wasn't struggling with performance, but with empathetic connections. "I don't know what's really happening in the team", he admitted. "It's like I'm managing activity, not people".

During deeper reflections, the real issue emerged: not remote work itself, but how fragmented interactions were the real challenge. Updates were flowing, but the larger shared context was missing. Conversations were punctual, but not long and thick. Small misunderstandings lingered. Subtle tensions went unaddressed.

What made the insight even more powerful was Michael's realisation that these challenges weren't limited to the pandemic era. Even into 2023 and 2024, this fragmentation of team interactions persisted. It became clear that remote working was not the cause—it had just accelerated a deeper shift. The newer ways of working and communicating in the digital age have fundamentally altered how teams connect, often leaving interactions more fragmented and disjointed. Short and snappy exchanges might be efficient, but were they also effective?

I encountered many such stories during my research, which pointed to a deeper insight: managing distributed teams grappling with fragmented interactions wasn't just a matter of coordination and alignment, it called for a new kind of leadership. When asked, respondents readily shared what this evolving leadership might require. While the specifics varied, one theme emerged consistently: the need for **leadership rooted in empathy**. A form of leadership that fosters connection, enables togetherness, and bridges the emotional gaps created by such fragmented interactions. It is this growing need for empathy in leadership, especially in the digital age, that we turn to next.

3.4 Greater Need for Empathy

Given the seniority of most executive coaching clients, my respondents were acutely aware of the leadership challenges their clients faced in navigating the changes brought on by digitalisation. These coaches suggested that leaders must not only recognise and manage the impact of digital transitions on their organisations, but also acknowledge the personal toll these changes were having on themselves and their teams.

In other words, the digital shift was not just an organisational issue happening "out there", it needed to be recognised as deeply personal. This recognition of the leader's own experience, separate from the structural transformation of the organisation, was cited as one of the key reasons for cultivating a more empathetic leadership approach—apart from the fact that it is the human thing to do. Just as leaders are navigating personal disruption, so are their teams. And in that shared vulnerability lies the need for compassion.

If this feels abstract, consider the story of a CEO tasked by the board with driving digital transformation. As the change unfolds, both the leader and their team will likely struggle, not just with the technical or strategic shifts, but with the human experience of disconnection. Fragmented interactions leave them unable to come together in meaningful or effective ways. In such a scenario, the role of empathy becomes clear, not as a soft skill, but as one which is critical. Crucially, an empathetic approach does not mean lowering the bar on accountability or delivery. Rather, in the context of digitally transforming organisations, empathy becomes a strategic asset, enabling connection, cohesion, and clarity in the face of complexity.

One coach captured this need particularly well by reflecting on the fundamentals of remote collaboration (an approach increasingly common in the digital age). He noted that in a virtual setting, without the informal moments, shared spaces, or everyday social cues that typically surround in-person work, conversations can quickly become purely transactional. "Interactions can so easily go very quickly into task because we've got no relationship frills around the edge here", he explained. In this context, emotional intelligence, empathy, and relational skills aren't optional extras, they become essential. With so many of the usual containers and connective tissue of workplace relationships stripped away, leaders need to bring more presence, sensitivity, and emotional attunement into their digital interactions.

Such a need has implications for the executive coaches. As one coach observed, "There will be a higher demand for executive coaches working with leaders on developing empathy—especially in settings where face-to-face interactions are no longer the norm". In a world where connection is increasingly mediated by screens, the ability to foster relational depth, read emotional cues, and lead with compassion becomes even more critical. Executive coaches are being called not just to support leaders in navigating organisational change, but to help them show up more fully and humanely in virtual spaces, where empathy is both harder to express and more essential than ever.

In this background, my research suggests that the coaching agenda needs to shift very quickly. There needs to be a stronger emphasis on helping leaders develop **empathy as a core capability**. Supporting emotional connection, relational trust, and human-centred leadership will need to become central to coaching conversations in the digital age. Watson et al. (2014) note that empathy is a critical active ingredient in leading through change. In times of significant disruption, such as digital transformation, an empathic approach can act as both a stabiliser and a catalyst. My research findings echo this perspective, and so do insights from some recent coaching literature.

Williams and Palmer (2020), studying coaching during the COVID-19 pandemic, found that individuals responded to the disruption in profoundly different ways. Klingenberg, writing in *Politico* (2020), suggested that the pandemic might compel us to reconsider "who we are and what we value". Palmer et al. (2020) highlight how themes like empathy, simplicity, connection, and health have begun to surface more frequently in coaching conversations. In my research, several coaches noted that clients were increasingly reflecting more deeply on personal meaning, identity, and well-being. As a result, many foresee a growing relevance of life and well-being coaching within executive practice.

This trend is also reflected in the ICF global study (2020), where over 60% of practitioners anticipated a rise in life vision and enhancement coaching in the post-pandemic world. Traditionally, executive coaching has focused on domains like leadership, performance, team dynamics, and career development. (Kilburgh, 2000; Peterson, 1996). Topics such as health, purpose, and inner alignment have often been categorised under life or wellness coaching (Cox et al., 2014). However, growing research suggests that executive coaching can play a far more holistic role, supporting not only outward success but also inner well-being (Cavanagh, 2006; Gabriel et al., 2014; Grant, 2020).

In the digitally evolving world, where disruption is both systemic and personal, empathy becomes the bridge, not just between people, but between performance and well-being. And as this bridge becomes more necessary, the coaching agenda must adapt and follow.

Reflective Exercise 3.1 Your Chosen Perspective

Take a moment to revisit the three lenses outlined in this chapter—The **functional** lens, which keeps tools and technology in focus, the **relational** lens, which is focused on interpersonal challenges in a video setup, and the **systemic** lens, which integrates the direct and indirect impact. These three lenses represent different ways coaches are making sense of digitalisation's impact. Now reflect on the following prompts: you may wish to write your responses, and as the next step, discuss them with a peer coach or supervisor.

1. Which perspective resonates most closely with your current coaching experience? What examples from your recent client sessions support this?
2. Which perspective feels least familiar or least developed in your thinking? Why might that be, and what might be the cost of overlooking it?
3. In your coaching conversations, which digitalisation themes do you tend to emphasise, tools, practice challenges, or wider contextual change?
4. How might your coaching shift if you began intentionally integrating one of the less familiar perspectives? What new questions might you bring into your sessions?

This exercise is not about choosing a "right" lens, but about expanding awareness. The more fluent we become in navigating these perspectives, the better equipped we are to coach meaningfully in a digitally evolving world.

Reflective Exercise 3.2 Empathy at the Core

As a coach, take a moment to reflect on the following questions.

1. Think of a leader you've coached recently.
   - In what ways were they grappling with digital change, organisationally and personally?
   - What emotions were unspoken but present?

2. How do you help clients lead with empathy in distributed or hybrid environments?
   - What tools, metaphors, or practices have worked?
   - What has been difficult or elusive?
3. Where in your coaching practice does empathy take a backseat, perhaps unintentionally?
   - What might shift if empathy was intentionally more central?
   - Are you modelling empathy in your own digital coaching presence?
4. How do you create a sense of connection and psychological safety when working virtually?
   - How attuned are you to subtle cues in your clients during online sessions?

Now pause and consider: What small but deliberate change could you make in your next session to elevate empathy, not as sentiment, but as a strategic resource?

References

Alavi, S., Abd. Wahab, D., Muhamad, N., & Arbab Shirani, B. (2014). Organic structure and organisational learning as the main antecedents of workforce agility. *International Journal of Production Research*, *52*(21), 6273–6295.

Baptista, J., Stein, M.-K., Klein, S., Watson-Manheim, M. B., & Lee, J. (2020). Digital work and organisational transformation: Emergent digital/human work configurations in modern organisations. *The Journal of Strategic Information Systems*, *29*(2), 101618.

Cavanagh, M. (2006). Mental-health issues and challenging clients in executive coaching. In D. R. Stober & A. M. Grant (Eds.), *Evidence-based coaching handbook: Putting best practices to work for your clients* (pp. 21–35). Wiley.

Cox, E., Bachkirova, T., & Clutterbuck, D. (2014). *The complete handbook of coaching*. Sage Publications.

Denzin, N. K. (2009). The elephant in the living room; or extending the conversation about the politics of evidence. *Qualitative Research*, *9*(2), 139–160.

Dewett, T., & Jones, G. R. (2001). The role of information technology in the organization: A review, model, and assessment. *Journal of Management*, *27*(3), 313–346.

Gabriel, A. S., Moran, C. M., & Gregory, J. B. (2014). How can humanistic coaching affect employee well-being and performance? An application of self-determination theory. *Coaching: An International Journal of Theory, Research and Practice*, *7*(1), 56–73.

Grant, A. M. (2020). A languishing–flourishing model of goal striving and mental health for coaching populations. In S. Palmer & A. Whybrow (Eds.), *Coaching researched: A coaching psychology reader* (pp. 65–82). Routledge.

Holstein, J. A., & Gubrium, J. F. (2007). Constructionist perspectives on the life course. *Sociology Compass*, *1*(1), 335–352.

ICF. (2020). *COVID-19 and the coaching industry*. https://coachingfederation.org/wp-content/uploads/2020/09/FINAL_ICF_GCS2020_COVID Study.pdf.

Kilburgh, R. (2000). *Executive coaching*. Amercian Psychological Association.

Lyytinen, K., Nickerson, J. V., & King, J. L. (2021). Metahuman systems= humans+ machines that learn. *Journal of Information Technology*, *36*(4), 427–445.

McAfee, A. (2006). Enterprise 2.0: The dawn of emergent collaboration. *Enterprise*, 2, 15–26.

Palmer, S., Panchal, S., & O'Riordan, S. (2020). Could the experience of the COVID-19 pandemic have any positive impact on wellbeing? *European Journal of Applied Positive Psychology*, *4*(10), 2397–7116.

Peterson, D. (1996). Executive coaching at work: The art of one-on-one change. *Consulting Psychology Journal*, *48*, 78–86.

Politico (Producer). (2020, 6 June). Coronavirus will change the world permanently. Here's how. www.politico.com/news/magazine/2020/03/19/coronavirus-effect-economy-life-society-analysis-covid-135579.

Riemer, K., Stieglitz, S., & Meske, C. (2015). From top to bottom. *Business & Information Systems Engineering*, *57*(3), 197–212.

Saunders, L. P., & Thornhill, A. (2019). *Research methods for business students*. Pearson Education.

Stray, V., Memon, B., & Paruch, L. (2020). A systematic literature review on agile coaching and the role of the agile coach. In P. Kuhrmann, K. Schneider, D. Pfahl, S. Amasaki, M. Ciolkowski, R. Hebig, P. Tell, J. Klünder, S. Küpper, & F. Münch (Eds.), *Product-focused software process improvement* (Lecture Notes in Computer Science, Vol. 12562, pp. 188–204). Springer.

Watson, J. C., Steckley, P. L., & McMullen, E. J. (2014). The role of empathy in promoting change. *Psychotherapy Research*, *24*(3), 286–298.

Williams, H., & Palmer, S. (2020). Coaching during the COVID-19 pandemic: Application of the CLARITY solution-focused cognitive behavioural coaching model. *International Journal of Evidence Based Coaching and Mentoring*, *18*(2), 204–214.

4 Experiencing Loss of Depth

The findings in this chapter build on the direct impact of digitalisation, the bottom arrow of the theoretical model shown in Figure 3.1. Most of my interviews took place during the height of the COVID-19 pandemic, a time when lockdowns and social distancing measures had abruptly shifted much of life online. Platforms like Zoom, Google Meet, Teams, BlueJeans, WebEx, and WhatsApp Video suddenly became the new spaces where we worked, learned, connected, and coached. The scale and speed of this transition from physical to virtual interaction were unprecedented, and its effects were deeply felt. It was therefore unsurprising that the move to virtual coaching, and the many challenges and discoveries it brought, emerged as one of the most prominent themes in my research conversations.

While the ICF (2020) study had already noted that some executive coaches were experimenting with virtual formats even before the pandemic, my research revealed that this sudden and complete transition impacted some respondents more significantly than others. Yet, regardless of where they began, most described a shared sense of loss when working virtually. This loss was not tied to any single factor but seemed to arise from an intricate interplay of changes. Three themes emerged most strongly from these conversations: the blurring of boundaries, a disturbed sense of presence, and the loss of physicality. Let us begin with the first, *the blurring of boundaries*.

4.1 Blurring of Boundaries

As suggested earlier, many coaches found the complete switch to virtual technology during the pandemic, considerably more challenging than expected. One key theme in these discussions of challenge was the blurring of boundaries between the physical and virtual worlds.

Executive coaches described two versions of this boundary erosion. The first is related to the always-on nature of their clients' professional

DOI: 10.4324/9781003638834-7

lives. Given the seniority of executive coaching clients, the digital age demanded constant connectivity, responding in real time to emerging organisational or industry developments. This unrelenting digital presence left little space for pause or reflection.

The second version emerged in the context of coaching sessions. Coaches observed that their already time-pressed clients now arrived at sessions straight from a series of back-to-back virtual meetings, often with no meaningful transition. Caleb captured this second shift poignantly when he remarked, "Clients no longer arrive, they appear [on screens]".

We are all familiar with the always-on nature of today's interconnected world. Our smartphones are rarely out of reach, and for senior leaders, the challenge is even more acute. Consider the sheer volume of communication they're expected to handle: while some emails can be triaged by a chief of staff, the list of stakeholders requiring a direct response from a CEO or CXO keeps growing. Board members, media, ESG activists, major investors, analysts, regulators, senior team members, and key government representatives, many of these expect real-time engagement, and the senior leader must often respond personally.

One of the central dilemmas in the knowledge economy is the lack of a clear, shared definition of productivity. In the absence of such clarity, busyness has become a proxy. Cal Newport (2016) explores this in great detail in his book, where he critiques the hustle culture that equates constant activity with effectiveness, and instead advocates for a more deliberate, reflective approach focused on meaningful results. While the suggested solutions couldn't be more appropriate, the reality is stark. Given the intensity of demands placed on today's top leaders, it seems unlikely that many will be able to reclaim time and space for reflection in a hurry. The solutions ask a lot from these already stretched leaders. The always-connected lifestyle is, in many cases, not even a choice, it's become embedded in the system, hence a massive challenge.

And it is exactly this challenge that many executive coaches raised when describing the blurring of boundaries in coaching conversations. One coach recalled pointing out to her client that checking her phone constantly, from waking to midnight, was neither natural nor healthy. What struck her was that the client had never even questioned this situation. The lure of productivity (or busyness), however misplaced, is so powerful that for many senior leaders, going without their phones or being unconnected for even 15 minutes feels unthinkable. But just because it is difficult, the leaders should not give up, and this is exactly where executive coaches need to step up and step in.

My research indicates that while this digitalised, hyper-connected way of living was already straining senior executives well before COVID-19, the pandemic amplified it. Paul's story, which follows, offers a vivid window into what that looks like in practice and, more importantly, how a seasoned coach can help senior leaders navigate through this challenge.

Always Connected, Never Present: Paul's Story (Case Study 3)

Paul, an experienced executive coach, shared a moment from a recent session with a senior woman leader in the tech industry. She was talented, articulate, and committed, but also visibly worn out.

"She told me she was going from one video call to the next with barely time to breathe, let alone think", Paul recalled. "Her calendar looked like a stack of bricks, solid, relentless, with no gaps".

What surfaced during the session was not just digital fatigue, but something deeper. Her personal and professional spaces had collapsed into one another. She would find herself replying to emails late into the night, fielding client calls from her bedroom, and attending meetings in a blur, sometimes forgetting whether the last one was a catch-up or a crisis.

"She said, 'It's just how things are now, right?', half-resigned, half-questioning", Paul noted.

It was a powerful moment. Because while the world around her had quietly declared this always-on, always-visible state as the new normal, her body and mind were sending different signals, exhaustion, confusion, and a subtle loss of self. That's where the coaching began in earnest.

While tempting to do, Paul didn't offer time management tips or quick fixes. Instead, he helped her pause, to notice the erosion of boundaries she had once carefully maintained. Together, they reflected on what presence meant for her, not just in meetings, but in her own life. They explored not just how to cope, but how to reclaim agency.

The key wasn't to adjust to the blur, but to notice how the real and virtual had merged, and then consciously redraw the lines.

Paul's story provides a great window into the blurring of boundaries for leaders, and an equally valuable lesson for executive coaches. It reminds us that when clients appear trapped in cycles of busyness, the coach's role is not to offer productivity hacks or calendar management tips, but to help them step back and see what has been lost in the blur. Paul's restraint and reflective stance exemplify how effective coaching begins not with doing more, but with noticing more.

For executive coaches, this story is a powerful example of what to do, and what to avoid, when working with overwhelmed senior leaders. It cautions against colluding with the client's pace or normalising exhaustion as ambition. Instead, it calls for creating spaces where clients can pause, reconnect with their own presence, and re-examine the choices shaping their boundaries. In such moments, coaching is all about *seeing*, and from that awareness, agency begins to return.

Paul's story also makes a mention of the second challenge, which Caleb had highlighted as the difference between clients "appearing" vs. "arriving". Many other coaches had highlighted the same concern of how, in today's virtual environment, clients often enter coaching sessions straight from other meetings, without any transition time. Clients often drop into virtual coaching sessions straight from back-to-back meetings, screens still glowing and thoughts scattered. What once existed as a natural buffer, a moment to pause, shift gears, and mentally prepare, has largely vanished.

Several coaches referred to this natural buffer as "journey time". Before the pandemic, the physical act of travelling to a coaching session, whether it was a long train ride, a short drive, or simply moving from a private office to a conference room to meet with the coach, offered clients invaluable reflective space. That transition time wasn't just logistical; it was psychological. It gave clients room to think, gather their thoughts, and transition into a more reflective mindset. And as most seasoned coaches know, the mindspace with which a client arrives can make a great difference to the quality of any coaching conversation.

With the move to virtual coaching, that space has quietly disappeared. As one coach put it, "we've lost that space because no one's travelling anymore". The absence of this buffer has subtly, but meaningfully, changed how clients enter, and often how they leave, coaching conversations.

With repeated references to blurred boundaries and the absence of clear transitions, a few executive coaches expressed a quiet but consistent wish: that their clients might regain some space for reflection, both before and after coaching sessions. In the context of senior leadership, where pressure and pace run high, coaches spoke with genuine concern. They cared deeply about their clients' well-being, and thus the loss of reflective time wasn't just a trivial issue, it was a troubling signal. The inability to pause, they felt, was not only affecting the quality of the coaching engagement but also impacting the quality of the client's overall professional and personal life.

Several coaches reflected that the core challenge both they and the client faced was, in essence, one of managing boundaries. One coach, trained in psychology, described it specifically as a classical "boundary issue", highlighting that a well-defined beginning and end to a coaching session is not merely procedural, but essential to maintaining depth and structure in the coaching conversation. With the pandemic and the rapid shift to virtual settings, these boundaries had become increasingly porous, for both clients and coaches. Many respondents described a shared sense of unease, noting how the blurring of work, life, and coaching spaces left them feeling disoriented. What surfaced was a common thread of discontent, not only with the changes themselves, but with a growing sense of diminished agency to restore the structure that once anchored their practice.

Interestingly, while many executive coaches spoke about these challenges, a smaller subset openly explored how these blurred boundaries were affecting them personally. In one memorable interview, a coach, Bhumi, paused mid-conversation to acknowledge that her next coaching session was scheduled back-to-back with our interview. She quickly added that it was far from ideal, and that she, too, needed to plan better, to build in reflective time between sessions, something she had just been lamenting as missing for her clients. In her own words, "I should give more time between meetings… but I've got to go in three minutes to start a coaching session, and I probably should've given myself a bit more time to go into that space. I'm going to arrive—boom. I've had no chance to reflect… I think that's a failing on my part, but that happens to the client, doesn't it?" Bhumi's comment was candid, and refreshingly self-aware. She went on to describe the need for what she called "journey time", the space between engagements that allows both coach and client to "come down, to think, to take stock, to process". Without it, she noted, reflection is compromised.

Bhumi's "coming down", Caleb's "arriving", and others' references to "journey time" all point to a deeper truth: in the digital age, boundary management is a shared challenge. Coaches weren't just observing it in clients, they were living it themselves. The lack of setup and transition time wasn't only being imposed, it was also, inadvertently, being self-created.

In the list below, I offer a few simple tips that may help coaches reclaim some agency and restore the reflective transition time so central to effective and impactful coaching practice.

Reclaiming Reflective Transition Time: Eight Tips for Coaches

1. **Schedule Space Between Sessions**: Avoid back-to-back coaching appointments. Even 15–20 minutes between sessions can provide essential mental and emotional reset time for you and thus help your next client as well.
2. **Create a Simple Ritual to Mark the Start and End**: This could be as simple as taking three deep breaths, counting your fingers and toes (my favourite), stretching your arms, or mentally chanting your favourite mantra. These rituals signal a boundary and help you shift your presence intentionally.
3. **Use a Digital Buffer**: Set your calendar to automatically end meetings five minutes early, i.e., only schedule 25, 50 and 75-minute sessions. This gives you protected transition time without needing to manually adjust each appointment.
4. **Step Away from the Screen**: Physically moving, even a short walk, changing rooms, or a few minutes outdoors—helps break the visual and cognitive continuity of screen-based coaching. Your body registers the boundary even if your schedule doesn't.
5. **Check-In With Yourself, Not Just the Client**: Before you begin, take a moment to ask: *What do I need to be fully present?* A brief internal check can improve your focus and energy in the session.
6. **Use Visual Anchors or Coaching Objects**: Having a physical object on your desk, like a coaching stone, notepad, a Ganesha statue (my chosen anchor) or any symbolic item, can serve as a reminder to pause and reflect before jumping into the next task.

7. **Block Post-Session Debrief Time**: Don't just plan the coaching session, definitely plan 10–15 minutes afterwards for a personal reflection, taking notes (I try and do it for each coaching session of mine), or a brief voice memo to yourself. This enhances learning and preserves presence.
8. **Model Boundaries for Clients**: Gently invite your clients to also take a few minutes before sessions begin. This can be positioned not as formality but as respect for the work and space. Modelling boundaries supports them to do the same in their lives.

4.2 Disturbed Presence

Having explored the blurring of boundaries and some practical ways to navigate them, we now turn to one of the central findings of this research. The question: *What happens to presence when coaching moves online?* Before delving into what the data revealed about presence and the shifting dynamics of working alliances in virtual settings, it's worth pausing to trace how this idea has evolved within the coaching literature.

As early as 1999, Richard proposed a model of remote coaching, suggesting that "coaching can also include telephone sessions and even e-mail correspondence" (1999, p. 28). Nearly a decade later, Frazee (2008) found that 25% of executive coaches were already working with clients remotely. Her study highlighted early benefits—serving geographically dispersed clients, providing *just-in-time support*, and increasing access to expertise at *reduced costs*. While we'll revisit these advantages in the next chapter, what's worth noting here is that even in those early explorations, she was cautioning the coaches about one crucial aspect: *presence*. Her message was clear, ensure the interactions remain human and relational, or risk weakening the coaching relationship.

Most coaching scholars agree that a strong coach–client relationship, or what's often called the working alliance (De Haan, 2011; Greenson, 1965) is critical to coaching effectiveness (De Haan et al., 2011, 2016). So, it's no surprise that conversations about the digital medium often include questions of efficacy, depth, and the quality of this alliance. In fact, some scholars argue that establishing a robust working alliance may even be more important in virtual coaching, precisely because of the absence of physical and non-verbal cues (Berry, 2005; Ghods & Boyce, 2013), another topic we will return to shortly.

Berry (2005), in a study involving over a hundred coaches from counselling, psychology, and related fields, made a strong case for remote coaching. His follow-up research in 2011 found no significant difference between face-to-face and remote settings in terms of reported outcomes (Berry et al., 2011). However, these findings come with an important caveat: the studies relied on coach-reported data and retrospective memory, and the sample included practitioners from life, health, sports, family, and spiritual coaching, making their direct application to executive coaching somewhat limited.

In contrast, Charbonneau (2002) found that both coaches and clients rated face-to-face coaching as more effective than its remote counterparts. Ghods (2009) offered a different view, demonstrating that strong coaching relationships can indeed be built without physical proximity. Amidst these contrasting findings, McLaughlin (2013, pp. 9–10) proposed a balanced perspective, describing distance coaching as "inherently different" and urging coaches to deepen their understanding of its nuances.

It is this position that I find most resonant. Rather than debating whether video-based coaching is better or worse than in-person work, recognising it as a different modality opens up space for meaningful exploration. And the pandemic has moved this from a theoretical discussion to a practical reality. Video-based coaching is no longer an option, it's often the default. To remain effective and relevant, today's executive coaches must not only be familiar with platforms like Zoom, MS Teams, and Google Meet, they must also learn to cultivate presence through them. And it is in this context that one of the most interesting findings from my research emerged: the challenge of a disturbed presence.

Challenge of Disturbed Presence

As executive coaching moved into the virtual realm, the significant challenge of cultivating genuine presence through a screen became an everyday challenge. Caleb, an executive coach with a psychoanalytical background, captured this tension through a metaphor. Drawing from somatic and relational coaching traditions, he spoke of the presence he strives to create in his sessions, akin to "creating a warm bath with the client where we both explore". It's a rich metaphor, the kind that suggests comfort, safety, and immersion. But then he paused, and added, "The client and the bath are there, but the water feels just a little bit cold in this virtual interface". His words reflect something most coaches were experiencing. While the structure of the coaching sessions remained intact, and the client was present, the relational warmth felt much harder to generate through a screen. This is where the idea of *disturbed presence* begins to crystallise.

Presence, in the context of coaching, is a layered and nuanced phenomenon, not easily captured in conversation or defined through a single lens. Noon (2017) alludes to this complexity by describing presence as operating across three dimensions: *internal*, *external*, and *relational*. Its dynamic quality, shifting within the coach, within the client, and between them, adds yet another layer to its already multidimensional nature.

Among the many scholars who have explored the idea of presence, the one who, for me, brings the greatest clarity is Mary Beth O'Neill (2011). She invites executive coaches to bring their *signature presence* into the coaching space, shaped by their own "values, passion, creativity, emotions and discerning judgement" (2011, p. 19). This signature presence is described as a form of resourcefulness and authenticity that enables coaches to navigate the whirlwind their clients may bring, drawing on their own "strength, interests and eccentricities"(O'Neill, 2011, p. 20). Seen in this light, the metaphor of "creating a warm bath" resonates as a way of preparing and cultivating one's signature presence. Just as we each draw our baths differently, some with essential oils, some with foam, others with silence or music, executive coaches, too, have their own process, shaped by personal preferences and inner resources. The abrupt shift to an all-virtual setting had disrupted this carefully honed process for coaches like Caleb, leaving the water "just a little bit cold".

Caleb was deeply aware of this disturbance in his presence and, given his high awareness, was already trying some mitigating solutions. "I have to make a sustained effort to cultivate my presence. [What does it mean?] I have to feel my feet on the ground to remain embodied". Given the influence of the somatic tradition, where the human body is viewed as the space through which we experience emotions, moods, thoughts, perceptions, and intuition (Aquilina &

Strozzi-Heckler, 2018), it was unsurprising that Caleb described a sense of disembodiment in fully virtual settings. Interestingly, while recounting this experience to me, he repeatedly touched the screen and his desk with his hands, perhaps enacting, through gesture, the same grounding process he had described with his feet. This physical engagement appeared to serve as a way of reconnecting with his body in a disembodied digital space. This interaction with Caleb left me wondering whether other coaches, too, were grappling with challenges to presence, and what strategies they might be using to navigate or mitigate those disruptions.

I realised that the experience of *disrupted presence* in virtual coaching settings was echoed across a wide range of coaching styles. Coaches with a relational or somatic orientation often expressed a deep sense of disembodiment, describing how the shift to screen-based interactions limited their access to the full physical and emotional landscape of the coaching encounter. One coach noted that, in a virtual setting, the conversation tends to remain focused above the shoulders, missing the vital signals and felt sense that come from the rest of the body. This absence, he felt, muted not just the client's presence but their own ability to fully engage, sense, and respond. The interactions were like two disembodied beings floating across a digital world.

But the challenge of presence wasn't limited to those coaching from a somatic or relational tradition. Coaches who operated from a more cognitive or goal-oriented framework also described a sense of disconnection, though often using a less embodied language. Gloria, for instance, drew on a linguistic metaphor to describe her experience: "It's a little bit like I speak French and Italian... I can speak them relatively fluently... but I always try not to [coach in these] because I feel like something's numbed... although I can understand the conversation, I can't quite get the nuances in the same way I can't quite be in my own language in that space". Her struggle wasn't about the body per se, but about resonance, the subtle rhythm of human connection that feels altered on a screen.

Coaches reflected on "disturbed presence", as a feeling that something subtle yet essential had changed in how they showed up with their clients. Given that presence is a complex and deeply personal phenomenon, it was perhaps unsurprising that many turned to *metaphors* to make sense of their experience. Some spoke of a "disturbance in the energy space", some about a "cold bath", while others likened virtual coaching to "speaking in a non-native language", technically possible, yet somehow less fluent, less natural. Across these accounts, it was clear that coaching through a screen did not feel quite the same as being physically present with another person. This recurring sense of dissonance was widely shared, even if described differently. The use of metaphor offered an important window into this experience, highlighting not just what was lost, but also how hard it is to articulate presence when it is disrupted or diluted.

Glitch in the Matrix

According to metaphor theorists (Lakoff, 1993; Steen, 2011), a metaphor arises when we describe one thing in terms of another, requiring a kind of "stretch or twist for sense-making" (Vivitsou, 2019, p. 123). Extending the stretch and twist of respondent metaphors helped me visualise and understand the disturbance in coaching presence much better. While none of the respondents explicitly used cinematic metaphors, two popular cultural references helped make sense of their reflections. The idea of a "disturbance in the force" from *Star Wars* or a "glitch in the Matrix" from *The Matrix* seems to come closest in capturing the essence of what many were describing. Both metaphors evoke a sudden, hard-to-pinpoint disruption, an invisible shift that alters the entire field of experience. I offer these references here not as exaggerations, but as aids for the reader, to illustrate just how real, unsettling, and difficult to articulate this experience was for many coaches.

In *Star Wars*, the phrase "a disturbance in the force" signals that something fundamental, often imperceptible to most, is out of balance. It is felt, not seen. It alerts the Jedi to a rupture in the deeper fabric of connection that binds all living things. This metaphor resonates strongly with how coaches described their altered presence in virtual settings. They weren't referring to technical glitches or visible distractions, but to something subtler: a shift in emotional resonance, relational flow, or energetic attunement. Like the Jedi, they sensed that something had changed in the field, even if they couldn't immediately name or trace it.

Similarly, in *The Matrix*, the notion of a "glitch", a flicker, a loop, a moment that doesn't quite align with reality, serves as a signal that something beneath the surface is off. It is often experienced as a minor anomaly, but one that points to a larger distortion in the system. This captures the subtle but persistent way many coaches experienced the virtual space: as something just slightly out of sync. The conversation continued, the tools worked, but the intuitive flow, the seamlessness of presence, was disrupted. Like a glitch, it wasn't always visible or explainable, but it left an imprint on the quality of connection and the felt sense of being fully present.

For some coaches, presence was more than professional attunement, it was almost spiritual. Described as "knowing without knowing", a deep, unspoken connection, it carried a sense of being truly with the other, beyond words or techniques. This kind of presence, often easier to evoke in person, felt diluted in virtual settings. As I explored this topic deeper with my respondents and conversations unfolded, a fundamental reason was identified: the relative absence of subtle, embodied cues in a video-based coaching setup.

Fewer Cues, Missing Nuances

One of the less spoken yet significant challenges of virtual coaching is the narrowing of sensory bandwidth. In a face-to-face setting, much of what is exchanged between coach and client need not be spoken; it can be sensed. A glance held a second too long, the shift of posture, a dry throat cleared before a difficult admission, or even the subtle cues of warmth in a handshake. These cues, though rarely named, form the rich background against which presence is built and trust takes shape.

Michael, a coach who also works in German, offered a cultural metaphor for this phenomenon. Referring to a German expression *"Ich kann ihn nicht riechen"*—literally, "I can't smell him"—he explained how the inability to "smell" someone goes beyond the literal. In its everyday use, the phrase conveys a visceral disconnection to describe one's dislike of the person. While such strong reactions may be rare in a healthy coaching relationship, the phrase itself points to something deeper. In a face-to-face coaching, we engage with all our senses, not just the verbal and visual ones. Michael further described the sensory field available in a face-to-face coaching: "you can see people, you can hear people, you can smell people. You can touch people, you feel whether they're giving a strong pressure, whether their hands are sweaty, whether they're cold, warm". For him, these cues were not peripheral—they were central to creating empathy and understanding. In the absence of such cues, particularly in video-based coaching, he felt that something essential was lost. "I can sense much less in a virtual setting", he said and with an expression which shared his frustration.

One could argue that even with reduced sensory cues, coaching can still be effective. As early as 2005, Rossett and Marino (2005, p. 47) noted that "an e-coach goes further... In some cases, the entire relationship happens online, using IM with voice and even video...". They highlighted several advantages we've already touched upon, serving geographically dispersed clients, offering just-in-time support, and increasing access to expertise at reduced costs, and added two more: *going where the action is*, and *leveraging technology's potential to scale*. All these benefits will be revisited in the next chapter, which covers the benefits of virtual coaching and explores *the opening of new windows*.

A few years later, Boyce and Clutterbuck (2010), drawing on *media richness theory* (Daft & Lengel, 1986), assessed e-coaching technologies through dimensions such as *feedback immediacy*, *information transfer*, *multiplicity of cues*, *emotional expression*, and *message tailoring*. Unsurprisingly, face-to-face coaching emerged as the richest medium across most dimensions. However, their analysis also pointed to the unique strengths of asynchronous communication, particularly its ability to create *space for reflection* and *reduce power dynamics* in the absence of visual or tonal cues.

This framework serves as an important reminder that face-to-face is not always necessarily the best option. When chosen with intention, digital formats can open up new and valuable possibilities for coaching practice. A thoughtful, context-sensitive use of the right medium is critical. That said, more research is still needed, particularly on how different media influence coaching relationships, mutual trust, and outcomes. Given the widespread adoption of video-based communication across organisations, the luxury of choosing a preferred medium may no longer exist for many coaches. However, what remains firmly within a coach's control is the posture with which they approach these tools. An uncritical, automatic adoption—driven solely by client demand or prevailing trends, can create challenges that coaches may not have anticipated. The story of Paul, which follows, illustrates this point with striking clarity.

Fewer Cues, Missing Layers: Paul's Story (Case Study 4)

Paul, an experienced coach from the UK, recounted a powerful reflection where, over a period of 12 months, he coached a woman entrepreneur based in India. Their sessions had been entirely virtual, and over time, they had explored deep and emotionally charged issues, especially around her past work experiences and a lingering sense of loss. "We did some really meaningful work", Peter explained. "We explored why she felt stuck, her grief over leaving a previous role, and an underlying narrative about being a woman in her professional space".

The coaching felt rich and impactful. But something unexpected happened when they finally met in person. "It was extraordinary", Peter recalled. "Meeting her physically, seeing her full body, her energy, her 360-degree presence, was a surprise. She was vivacious, lively, and full of expressive gestures. That just hadn't come through on video".

Peter wasn't questioning the quality of their work together, but the moment left him reflective. "Would the coaching have been different if I had seen that version of her earlier? I have no clue", he admitted. "But it made me realise how much nuance might be missed when our senses are narrowed to just a screen".

His story reminds us that even when coaching feels deep, virtual settings can sometimes offer only a partial window into the client's world. This doesn't make video coaching ineffective, but it does invite coaches to remain mindful of what might be just outside the frame.

Unlike Paul, who was able to build a strong connection despite the digital setting, many other coaches were less certain that they could form a robust working relationship through a screen. One coach went so far as to say, the "idea of the relationship being a unique human quality is, as far as I'm aware, not something we can easily recreate digitally and through a computer". This relational foundation, often referred to as the *working alliance* (Berry et al., 2011; Graßmann et al., 2020) is widely recognised as critical to executive coaching success (De Haan et al., 2011, 2020). Any challenge in building or sustaining this alliance warrants serious attention. Empathy and intuition are among a coach's most valuable tools in this process, and both can be strained in virtual settings, where cues are fewer and signals fainter.

Gloria expanded on her metaphor of coaching in a foreign language to describe how her intuition felt muted in a virtual setting. “It’s the nuances”, she explained, “the little things you would notice if it were your mother tongue, things you can’t quite express or hear or pick up when it’s another language, even if you’re fluent”. For her, virtual coaching numbed her intuition.

Across the interviews, it became clear that not all coaches named this issue in the same way, but many touched upon it. Some spoke directly about the quality of the relationship, others described a struggle to fully understand the client’s emotional state. A few mentioned missing nuances, while others reflected on the sense of having only a partial view of the client. Though the language varied, a common thread ran through these reflections: a recognition that virtual coaching often involves fewer cues. Several coaches went further, observing that in the absence of sensory cues, they had to work harder, stretching their attention, tuning in more deliberately, and compensating for what wasn’t visible or audible. At the time of my research, the concept of “Zoom fatigue” was still emerging in academic literature. But studies since have confirmed what these coaches were pointing to: the cognitive and emotional strain of sustained virtual engagement is real (Bergmann et al., 2023; Luebstorf et al., 2023; Tawadros, 2024).

Across these distinct studies, a coherent thread can be located. While studying “Zoom fatigue”, Luebstorf et al. (2023) highlighted how virtual environments generate stress, from camera fatigue to blurred home-office boundaries, requiring adaptive coping strategies. Tawadros’s (2024) exploration of video-mediated coaching revealed that clients notice shifts in presence, rapport, and the spatial dynamics of the coaching relationship. The study by Bergmann et al. (2023) introduced a multifaceted framework: coaches experienced both a loss of depth and physicality in virtual sessions. Together, these studies underscore the challenge coaches face in building a strong working alliance with fewer available cues.

While many coaches shared that effective coaching is still possible despite these constraints, it’s important to remain aware of the limitations. As one coach observed, what is seen and heard forms only half the work, the rest depends on subtle sensing, which is diminished online. Another pointed out that even visual cues are partial, with only a head-and-shoulder frame visible in most setups. Unlike in-person settings where full-body presence enriches perception, virtual coaching often requires extra, and sometimes unconscious, effort to compensate for what is missing.

It helps to step back for a moment and remember that we, as humans, weren't built for this. As one of the coaches I spoke with put it simply: "We [are not] wired to communicate on Zoom". Her words echo something deeper than just fatigue, they point to our *evolutionary inheritance*. For most of human history, we made sense of our world by sitting together, sharing stories across a fire. The warmth of presence, the rhythm of voice, the flicker of a glance, all of it mattered. Face-to-face wasn't a format; it was the default. And while the modern world has given us screens, headphones, and high-definition video, it hasn't rewired those deeper instincts. We can even say that coaching, at its heart, has always been a kind of modern-day fire, a space where stories are heard, reflected, and reimagined. In virtual coaching, we are now engaging through a narrow window. Gestures are cropped, silences feel different, and the invisible signals we once relied on, breath, posture, pace, are softened or lost entirely.

Of course, coaching can still happen. As many coaches affirmed, meaningful work is possible, even powerful, through digital mediums. But it comes at a cost. There is a big and often tiring compensatory effort, sometimes conscious, often not, where we lean in harder, concentrate more, and try to piece together the parts that would have once spoken for themselves. It's not just screen fatigue, it's evolutionary friction.

To be clear, this is not nostalgia for a lost past. It's simply a recognition that even as our tools evolve rapidly, our wiring does not. And so, in a digital world of coaching, one of the most human things we can do is acknowledge what's missing, and then, with care and skill, work to bridge that gap.

4.3 Absent Physicality

In a few of the interviews, coaches found themselves reaching for something that went beyond the already discussed missing cues or relational shifts of virtual coaching. Often, the conversations about presence veered into the absence of *physicality*.

The example of Willow gives a good background to what is meant by this physicality and how it differs from the other sensory and presence challenges. Willow, who is part-owner of a coaching and HR advisory firm, reflecting on her experience of virtual coaching, drew a parallel from her everyday life. She noticed how the younger members of her family seemed increasingly absorbed in screens, always connected, yet somehow less physically present. That same concern found its way into her coaching reflections. It wasn't just that she couldn't read a client's body language fully or pick up subtle shifts in energy. It was the very *material absence* of being in the same space.

Part of Willow's unease echoed the themes already explored, but there was also something else in her reflection, something more grounded, more physical. She was speaking not just of presence, but of *physicality*. Of the small, tangible acts that carry meaning precisely because they are done in the same space, with the same air, on the same floor. She spoke of wanting to reach out and place a reassuring hand on a client's arm. Offering a box of tissues at the right moment. Of sliding a glass of water across the table during a long reflective pause. These were not grand gestures, but they were *materially real*, anchored in physical co-presence. They were, in a way, gestures of care through matter: hand, object, space.

At one level, such gestures could be viewed as tools that help strengthen the coaching relationship. But to stop there would miss something essential. Their impact doesn't just lie in their symbolic value, they carry a *felt weight* because they are physical acts, grounded in the material world. The texture of a tissue, the sound of a glass being placed on a wooden table, the embodied silence that emerges when two people sit in the same room, all of this contributes to a very unique experience of coaching.

Several coaches spoke about the physical environment they used to create for their clients, not just as a backdrop, but as an intentional, curated space that held meaning. One coach described how, in face-to-face sessions, she would welcome clients into a meeting room, offer them a cup of tea or coffee, and take time to settle in before the conversation began. These small acts, she said, felt like part of "looking after" her clients. It wasn't just about hospitality—it was an embodied way of saying, *you are safe here, this space is for you*. Another coach shared how many of his clients were extremely busy people for whom the monthly coaching session might be the only time carved out for self-reflection. He described making the physical environment intentionally inviting, a calm, contained space that allowed clients to slow down. For him, coaching wasn't just about time, it was also about space. A sanctuary, of sorts.

While these reflections could be interpreted through the lens of control, an attempt by the coach to manage the setting or hold symbolic authority, neither coach spoke from a place of power. What came through instead was care. A quiet, grounded desire to support the client not just through words, but through the physical experience of being held in a thoughtfully created space.

For some coaches, the idea of physical space wasn't incidental, it was ritualised into their practice. The coaching relationship didn't begin with a scheduled Zoom call; it began in carefully chosen physical environments designed to support depth and reflection. One coach described how her process always started with a one- or two-day face-to-face retreat, where she and the client would explore a wide range of themes before arriving at a formal coaching agenda. Another coach, who often worked with senior leaders, insisted on beginning the engagement only after spending a full day and a half offsite with the client, walking, talking, sometimes sharing a meal or a drink. For them, it wasn't just about the time, it was about where that time was spent.

The physical settings, retreat venues, outdoor cafés, quiet corners, were part of the coaching process itself. Now, that space had collapsed into a screen. The rich, sensory environment and holding spaces of the past had been replaced by curated Zoom backgrounds and strategically arranged bookshelves. The rituals that once involved shared physical presence were now flattened into pixels and camera angles. In virtual settings, holding becomes more abstract. The carefully prepared tea, the weight of a door closing behind the client, the warmth of the chair across the room, all of it dissolves into pixels. And with it, something human and material is lost.

Yet, as some coaches pointed out, the shift also brought something unexpected. While they could no longer shape the physical environment in which the coaching took place, they now found themselves with a *window* into the client's world. With blurred boundaries, coaching often unfolded in home offices, spare bedrooms, or makeshift workspaces. For the first time, coaches could see the shelves behind the client, the family photos, the cat passing through the frame. This reversal,where the client's space became visible, and the coach's space became fixed, was unfamiliar territory. Many viewed this as an opening, an opportunity to engage with new kinds of spaces, and perhaps even to reimagine what a coaching environment could be.

Given the detailed discussions around disturbed presence, weakened working alliances, missing cues, lost nuances, absent physicality, and coach fatigue, it might feel that respondents were uniformly critical of virtual coaching. But that was not the case. Even those who voiced strong concerns about the challenges of working in a virtual setting were mindful of its inevitability, and open to what it might offer. As the previous paragraph suggests, while acknowledging what is lost, many also hinted at what might be gained. And so, having explored the constraints, let's now turn our attention to the possibilities, how virtual coaching opens new windows when approached with awareness, skill, and creativity.

Reflective Exercise 4.1 Evaluating Your Transition Practices as a Coach

Having reviewed the practical suggestions for reclaiming reflective transition time listed at the end of section 4.1, this exercise invites you to critically evaluate your current practices. The aim is not to prescribe a right way of working, but to enhance awareness of how your coaching presence is shaped by the moments before, between, and after sessions. Consider the following questions:

1. **Session Entry**: How do you typically prepare for a coaching session? Do you have a consistent approach to becoming mentally and emotionally available before the session begins?
2. **Session Exit**: What processes, if any, do you follow to close a session, for yourself and for your client? How do you ensure that the conversation is meaningfully concluded rather than abruptly ended?

3. **Transition Awareness**: Do you consciously create space between coaching sessions or other work commitments? How does the absence or presence of this space affect your ability to be fully present?
4. **Boundary Clarity**: To what extent are your professional boundaries—physical, temporal, and psychological—clear and respected in your current coaching schedule?
5. **Self-Modelling**: Are you modelling the kind of boundary-conscious behaviour you encourage in your clients? In what ways might your current approach reinforce or contradict the values you bring to your coaching?

Now take a few minutes to document your responses. **Identify one small adjustment you could make in your scheduling, preparation, or closure rituals** that could support a more intentional and grounded coaching practice.

Reflective Exercise 4.2 Naming the Disturbance

Presence, especially in virtual spaces, can be hard to articulate, and even harder to notice when it's disrupted. Metaphors can offer a bridge between what we feel and what we can say. Take a moment to reflect on your own experience of coaching in virtual settings and complete the following exercise:

- Think back to a coaching session, recent or distant, where something felt off, even if everything appeared to be working on the surface. What was the nature of that disruption? How did you notice it? Through energy? Body sensation? Disconnection?
- If you had to choose a metaphor to describe that moment, what would it be? Is it like a *glitch*, a *disturbance*, a *blurring*, or something entirely different? Why does that image or metaphor fit for you?

Write your reflections, sketch an image, or even invent your own metaphor for presence. Often, what we can name, we begin to understand.

Reflective Exercise 4.3 Mapping Your Sensory Presence in Virtual Coaching

In this four-step exercise, you are invited to pause and reflect on how your presence, as a coach, is expressed, experienced, and perhaps constrained in virtual settings. The aim here is not to judge, but to build awareness. Think of it as tuning your instrument before the next coaching session. After all, in coaching, we use the self as the primary instrument for change. And like any instrument, its effective use depends on three conditions: *understanding it*, *caring for it*, and *checking it* regularly for *quality* and *sensitivity* (Bachkirova, 2016).

Step 1: Self-Audit—Presence Across Senses: In virtual coaching, some sensory inputs naturally narrow, others may need intentional strengthening. This step helps you become aware of what you're tuning into and what might be fading out. Use Table 4.1 for each of the **seven dimensions**; reflect and jot down:

1. What you typically notice in a coaching session.
2. What feels limited, missing, or altered (if anything) when working virtually?
3. One thing you would stop or start doing to strengthen that particular dimension.

The text filled in the table is to be viewed as just a prompt to aid reflections.

Table 4.1 Plotting Presence Across Senses

Dimension of Presence	What You Usually Notice	What Feels Limited or Missing in Virtual Coaching	One Small Practice to Stay Connected to This Sense
1. Sight (Visual cues)	*e.g., facial expressions, gestures*	*e.g., limited field of view, camera angle*	*e.g., ask clients to adjust framing, look into the client's eyes and not the camera*
2. Sound (Tone, pace, silence)	*e.g., voice modulation, pauses*	*e.g., video and audio lag, missing tone subtleties*	*e.g., use headphones, lean into pauses*
3. Touch / Embodiment	*e.g., hand-shake, seating posture*	*e.g., no tactile feedback, body cues missing*	*e.g., ground yourself physically before and during sessions*

(*Continued*)

Table 4.1 Cont

Dimension of Presence	What You Usually Notice	What Feels Limited or Missing in Virtual Coaching	One Small Practice to Stay Connected to This Sense
4. Smell / Atmosphere	*e.g., room feel, presence, warmth*	*e.g., loss of ambient sense*	*e.g., light a candle or build a familiar scent ritual in your space*
5. Intuition (Gut sense, subtle knowing)	*e.g., felt sense of client state*	*e.g., feels muted or numbed*	*e.g., pause and ask "What's going on beneath the surface?"*
6. Energy / Relational Field	*e.g., the "vibe" in the room*	*e.g., flattened or delayed connection*	*e.g., acknowledge shifts in energy explicitly*
7. Movement / Rhythm	*e.g., pacing of interaction, fidgeting*	*e.g., constrained visibility, reduced flow*	*e.g., observe your own rhythm, allow intentional stillness*

Step 2: Zooming In, Your Signature Presence: Think about one recent virtual session that felt powerful.

- What helped you feel most present?
- What did you do (before, during, or after) that supported your depth?
- What do you remember sensing, not just hearing or seeing?

Write a short reflection here:

🖉 *What supported your signature presence in that session?*

____

____

____

🖉 *What elements of presence felt muted or missing?*

____

____

____

____

Step 3: Designing Your Sensory Anchor: Based on your responses above, identify one small ritual or practice you can introduce to help deepen your presence in the next three virtual sessions. Choose from the examples below, or design your own. A few examples to aid the reflection are listed below.

- Use a physical object (stone, candle, artefact) as a visual and tactile anchor.
- Begin with a three-minute grounding ritual (breath, body scan, posture check).
- Adjust camera height to simulate eye-level contact and presence.
- Use silence more intentionally in sessions.

✐ *My new practice to support deeper virtual presence*:

____

____

____

____

Step 4: Closing Reflection: After your next virtual coaching session, revisit this page and jot down:

✐ *What felt different?*

____

____

✐ *What worked or didn't?*

____

____

✐ *What will you keep, drop, or adapt going forward?*

____

____

____

____

This exercise is not a one-time reflection, it's a mirror you can return to. Because coaching in the digital age demands not just better tools, but deeper presence. And often, presence begins with noticing what's missing.

References

Aquilina, E., & Strozzi-Heckler, R. (2018). Somatic coaching. In S. Palmer & A. Whybrow (Eds.), *Handbook of coaching psychology* (2nd ed., pp. 229–240). Routledge.

Bachkirova, T. (2016). *The self of the coach: Conceptualization, issues, and opportunities for practitioner development* (Vol. 68). Educational Publishing Foundation.

Bergmann, R., Rintel, S., Baym, N., Sarkar, A., Borowiec, D., Wong, P., & Sellen, A. (2023). Meeting (the) pandemic: Videoconferencing fatigue and evolving tensions of sociality in enterprise video meetings during COVID-19. *Computer Supported Cooperative Work (CSCW)*, *32*(2), 347–383.

Berry, R. M. (2005). *A comparison of face-to-face and distance coaching practices: The role of the working alliance in problem resolution*. Georgia State University.

Berry, R. M., Ashby, J. S., Gnilka, P. B., & Matheny, K. B. (2011). A comparison of face-to-face and distance coaching practices: Coaches' perceptions of the role of the working alliance in problem resolution. *Consulting Psychology Journal: Practice and Research*, *63*(4), 243.

Boyce, L. A., & Clutterbuck, D. (2010). E-coaching: Accept it, it's here, and it's evolving! In G. Hernez-Broome & L. A. Boyce (Eds.), *Advancing executive coaching: Setting the course for successful leadership coaching* (pp. 285–315). Wiley.

Charbonneau, M. (2002). *Participant self-perception about the cause of behavior change from a program of executive coaching*. Unpublished doctoral dissertation, Alliant International University, Los Angeles, CA.

Daft, R. L., & Lengel, R. H. (1986). Organizational information requirements, media richness and structural design. *Management Science*, *32*(5), 554–571.

De Haan, E. (2011). *Relational coaching: Journeys towards mastering one-to-one learning*. John Wiley & Sons.

De Haan, E., Culpin, V., & Curd, J. (2011). Executive coaching in practice: What determines helpfulness for clients of coaching? *Personnel Review*, *40*(1), 24–44. doi:10.1108/00483481111095500.

De Haan, E., Grant, A. M., Burger, Y., & Eriksson, P.-O. (2016). A large-scale study of executive and workplace coaching: The relative contributions of relationship, personality match, and self-efficacy. *Consulting Psychology Journal: Practice and Research*, *68*(3), 189–207. doi:10.1037/cpb0000058.

De Haan, E., Molyn, J., & Nilsson, V. O. (2020). New findings on the effectiveness of the coaching relationship: Time to think differently about active ingredients? *Consulting Psychology Journal: Practice and Research*, *72*(3), 155.

Frazee, R. V. (2008). *E-coaching in organizations: A study of features, practices, and determinants of use*. University of San Diego.

Ghods, N. (2009). *Distance coaching: The relationship between the coach-client relationship, client satisfaction, and coaching outcomes*. Alliant International University, Marshall Goldsmith School of Management.

Ghods, N., & Boyce, C. (2013). Virtual coaching and mentoring. In J. Passmore, D. B. Peterson, & T. Freire (Eds.), *The Wiley-Blackwell handbook of the psychology of coaching and mentoring* (pp. 501–523). Wiley-Blackwell.

Graßmann, C., Schölmerich, F., & Schermuly, C. C. (2020). The relationship between working alliance and client outcomes in coaching: A meta-analysis. *Human Relations*, *73*(1), 35–58.

Greenson, R. R. (1965). The working alliance and the transference neurosis. *The Psychoanalytic Quarterly*, *34*(2), 155–181.

ICF. (2020). 2020 ICF global coaching study: Executive summary. https://coachfederation.org/app/uploads/2020/09/FINAL_ICF_GCS2020_ExecutiveSummary.pdf.

Lakoff, G. (1993). The contemporary theory of metaphor. The contemporary theory of metaphor. In A. Ortony (Ed.), *Metaphor and thought* (2nd ed., pp. 202–251). Cambridge University Press.

Luebstorf, S., Allen, J. A., Eden, E., Kramer, W. S., Reiter-Palmon, R., & Lehmann-Willenbrock, N. (2023). Digging into "zoom fatigue": A qualitative exploration of remote work challenges and virtual meeting stressors. *Merits*, *3*(1), 151–166.

McLaughlin, M. (2013). Less is more: The executive coach's experience of working on the telephone. *International Journal of Evidence Based Coaching & Mentoring*, *S7*, pp. 1–13.

Newport, C. (2016). *Deep work: Rules for focused success in a distracted world*. Hachette UK.

Noon, R. (2017). *Exploring presence in executive coaching conversations*. Oxford Brookes University.

O'Neill, M. B. (2011). *Executive coaching with backbone and heart: A systems approach to engaging leaders with their challenges*. John Wiley & Sons.

Richard, J. T. (1999). Multimodal therapy: A useful model for the executive coach. *Consulting Psychology Journal: Practice and Research*, *51*(1), 24.

Rossett, A., & Marino, G. (2005). If coaching is good, then e-coaching is. *T AND D*, *59*(11), 46.

Steen, G. J. (2011). The contemporary theory of metaphor—now new and improved! *Review of Cognitive Linguistics*, *9*(1), 26–64.

Tawadros, T. (2024). Video-mediated coaching. In J. Passmore, S. J. Diller, S. Isaacson, & M. Brantl (Eds.), *The digital and AI coaches' handbook* (pp. 89–100). Routledge.

Vivitsou, M. (2019). Digitalisation in education, allusions and references. *CEPS Journal*, *9*(3), 117–136.

5 Opening of New Windows

5.1 Advantages of Virtual Coaching

Before we move into the exciting world of virtual coaching and new spaces, it would be helpful to revisit what the literature tells us about the advantages of virtual coaching. While much of the last chapter of this book has focused on the disruptions and losses brought on by digitalisation, thus helping the practice evolve, it would be incomplete, and perhaps unfair, to overlook the genuine advantages that virtual formats have introduced. Some of these have been touched upon in the earlier sections, but the topic merits a detailed discussion.

Scholars (Frazee, 2008; Richard, 1999; Rossett & Marino, 2005) and practitioners (Virtual Executive Coaching, 2025) alike have highlighted a number of benefits of virtual connections to support executive coaching. These range from increased accessibility and cost-efficiency to greater scheduling flexibility and reach across geographies. Even before the COVID-19 pandemic forced a global pivot to digital platforms, some early researchers were pointing to the promise of e-coaching as more than just a substitute for face-to-face interaction. They saw it as a meaningful evolution in its own right, opening doors to timely support, broader inclusion, and new models of engagement. The term *e-coaching*, initially used to define remote or technology-mediated coaching (Berry, 2005; Frazee, 2008), has continued to evolve alongside advancements in communication technologies. Geissler et al. (2014) built on earlier definitions by emphasising the replacement of face-to-face interaction with modern media, and outlined four specific formats through which e-coaching could take place: "(1) audio communication (telephone), (2) video communication, (3) synchronous text-based communication, and (4) asynchronous text-based communication" (p. 166).

DOI: 10.4324/9781003638834-8

Around the same period, Ghods and Boyce (2013), in a comprehensive literature review, highlighted the limited academic attention given to e-coaching. Drawing on parallels from e-mentoring and online counselling, they note that while there were growing examples of virtual practice, the research base for executive coaching remained sparse. For instance, the 2011 Sherpa Executive Coaching Survey showed that 30% of coaches were already using technology in some form, a figure that rose to 39% by 2015 (Sherpa Coaching, 2015). So, in practice, coaches had begun integrating virtual platforms by the early 2000s, but scholarship was slow to catch up.

This imbalance between practice and research has seen only modest correction over the past decade, though there are signs of more sustained engagement with the topic (Bajpai & Clutterbuck, 2024; Geissler et al., 2014; Kanatouri, 2020; Kanatouri & Geissler, 2017; Passmore et al., 2024). It is worth noting that this observation excludes the more recent surge of research emerging in the realm of AI in coaching. That particular uptick seems to mirror a broader trend across disciplines, where anything labelled "AI" is quickly attracting scholarly attention and institutional enthusiasm.

During my research, many practitioners pointed to the obvious and well-established advantages of virtual coaching. These were often shared without hesitation, as if their value was already assumed. For instance, Divya noted, "Even before COVID, I had lots of multinational companies as clients. I was conducting the majority of my coaching sessions through video calls", highlighting the clear advantage of geographical reach. Kylie admitted, "I was totally against video-based coaching [earlier]. Now I can't imagine wasting three hours commuting for a 90-minute session,not to mention the cost savings". For her, efficiency had become a decisive benefit. Another coach, Brian, offered a broader view, observing that "technology can be surprisingly democratic", referencing how digital formats can open access to coaching for those previously excluded by cost or location. Given that many of these benefits are both self-evident and well-researched (Doolittle, 2022; Ghods & Boyce, 2013; Michalik & Schermuly, 2024; Schermuly et al., 2022; Tavis & Woodward, 2024), and that the more interesting topic of *newer coaching spaces* is discussed in section 5.3, I won't dwell on them any further. Instead, through Table 5.1, I summarise the core benefits of virtual coaching along with enabling technological elements for the reader's reference and reflection.

Table 5.1 Benefits of Virtual Coaching and Enabling Tech

Benefits of Virtual Coaching	*Enabling Technology or Digital Element*
1. Accessibility across geographies and time zones	Video conferencing platforms (e.g., Zoom, Teams); Asynchronous tools (email, messaging apps)
2. Scheduling flexibility and reduced logistical overhead	Online scheduling tools, calendar integrations, and location-independent access via mobile devices
3. Cost-effectiveness for clients and organisations	Elimination of travel and venue costs
4. Opportunities for just-in-time or on-demand coaching	Instant messaging, voice notes, and flexible video call functionality on smartphones
5. Broader inclusion and reach	Digital platforms with lower entry barriers; no restrictions to connect across countries
6. Increased efficiency for time-pressed clients	Shorter, focused virtual sessions are possible; flexible formats (e.g., 30-minute drop-ins)
7. Scalability for organisational coaching programmes	Integrated coaching platforms with dashboards, reporting, and multi-coach coordination
8. Reduced environmental footprint	Remote work eliminates the need for travel or printed materials

5.2 Pandemic Impact

Nearly three decades ago, management thinker Drucker (1993) declared that "commuting to office work is obsolete". Yet, as recently as 2019, that vision had not fully materialised, given that half of global organisations still did not support remote work (Labs, 2019). Reflecting on this, Adam Grant (2020) noted that Drucker's prophecy might remain unfulfilled forever,until the world changed overnight. As the pandemic unfolded, millions of people were suddenly working from home, and Grant thus had to modify his position and suggest that "the world of work would never be the same again". I would go one step further: it's not just the world of work that will never be the same again, the world of executive coaching has been irrevocably altered too. The pandemic didn't introduce the benefits of virtual coaching (Section 5.1); it simply accelerated their adoption, making them more visible, more necessary, and, in many cases, more permanent. We can identify five specific areas where pandemic-induced change had significant positive implications for executive coaching practice. Let us briefly explore each of them.

Changing Coaching Agendas: Well-Being, Purpose, and the Search for Meaning

The pandemic, as Klingenberg observed, has prompted many of us to reconsider "who we are and what we value" (Politico, 2020). This period of disruption didn't just alter routines, it nudged people into deeper reflection. For many coaching clients, the questions that surfaced weren't only about performance or promotion, but about meaning, connection, and the shape of their lives. Executive coaching, long associated with leadership, career development, and high performance, began to see a shift in tone. Clients increasingly brought in themes that might once have been relegated to life coaching or wellness spaces, topics like simplicity, balance, health, and emotional well-being (Palmer et al., 2020). These weren't fleeting concerns. They pointed to a deeper realignment in what clients sought from coaching. This shift was also mirrored in the ICF's global research. In one study, over 60% of both coaches and business professionals predicted a rise in demand for life vision and enhancement coaching in the post-pandemic era (ICF, 2020). A multi-country study by Jarosz (2021), including participants from China (Wuhan), the US, UK, and Spain during the early pandemic, highlighted rising anxiety, distraction, and a sense of lost control among employees. Though limited in scale, the study found that coaching helped improve both well-being and performance, reinforcing its value as a support mechanism in times of crisis.

Return of the Expert: Rediscovering the Value of Expertise

Nicholas (2017) had earlier criticised the growing dismissal of expertise and the rise of anti-intellectual sentiment in public discourse. But the pandemic, he now suggests, may have reversed some of that trend, renewing public appreciation for expert voices in times of uncertainty (Politico, 2020). In this climate, the value placed on professional credentials, experience, and evidence-based guidance has resurged. Although awareness of coaching qualifications and accreditations among the general public remains uneven (Lancaster & Smith, 2002), executive coaches are widely perceived as experts, especially by their clients (A. M. Grant, 2005, 2006). If the broader societal shift towards trusting expertise holds, it is likely to enhance the perceived legitimacy and demand for executive coaching. As Lawrence notes, professions that help, healthcare workers, caregivers, psychologists, may all see renewed respect in the post-pandemic world (Politico, 2020). Executive coaching, with its strong relational and developmental orientation, stands to benefit from this shift.

Coaching Steps Up: Organisational Optimism and a Spirit of Service

The ICF's global survey during the pandemic revealed cautious optimism within the coaching community. Over 75% of coaches believed that coaching would play a larger role within organisations in the following six months (ICF, 2020), a signal that investment in executive coaching might rebound as the world transitions into a post-pandemic phase. At the same time, a different kind of trend began to emerge, one rooted less in market forces and more in collective ethos. Between half and two-thirds of coaches reported offering pro-bono coaching during the pandemic (ICF, 2020). Whether this was a response to reduced business or a sense of purpose, it reflected something deeper: a recognition that coaching had something to offer in a moment of global stress. Many coaches stepped up, not just to sustain their practice, but to serve. This movement towards pro-bono work may have helped popularise coaching, bringing it to individuals and communities who may not otherwise have accessed it.

Tech as a Coaching Partner: Navigating New Frontiers

One of the more tangible shifts accelerated by the pandemic was the widespread embrace of digital technology in coaching. The ICF's (2020) survey conducted during the pandemic found that most coaches felt they had adequate technology to continue delivering sessions effectively during the crisis. Given that most coaching engagements require only a stable video conferencing platform, such as Zoom, Teams, or Google Meet, this readiness isn't surprising. Yet, beyond mere adequacy, the pandemic opened up new possibilities. Coaches and clients alike grew more comfortable with digital mediums, and coaching research has long noted that this comfort with technology can significantly shape coaching outcomes (Boyce & Clutterbuck, 2010; Pascal et al., 2015). As virtual communication continues to expand within organisations, new platforms and tools will likely emerge, reshaping how coaching is delivered and experienced. Looking ahead, coaching management systems may evolve to incorporate features like virtual or mixed reality, further blurring the boundaries between presence and distance. In this evolving landscape, digital fluency is no longer optional, it is becoming a core capability for executive coaches. While the pandemic forced a rapid adaptation, it may have also seeded long-term innovation, positioning technology not as a barrier but as a creative partner in the coaching relationship.

Learning Never Locked Down: The CPD Surge

One of the quieter yet significant shifts during the pandemic was the surge in continuous professional development (CPD) among coaches. The ICF (2020) survey noted that many coaches increased their CPD hours during this period. While the exact drivers remain unclear, a combination of factors likely played a role: reduced coaching hours, more flexible schedules, and the widespread availability of online CPD offerings, often at lower or no cost. Importantly, coaches seem to believe that the changes brought about by the pandemic are here to stay. Over 60% indicated that coaching would not return to pre-pandemic norms. In this context, the rise in CPD reflects more than just available time, it signals a proactive effort to adapt, upskill, and stay relevant in a rapidly changing environment.

While coaching bodies are still evolving their guidance for the post-pandemic world, examples from adjacent fields offer useful clues. The International Psychoanalytic Association (IPA), for instance, has issued detailed recommendations on how to adapt remote sessions, including technical setup and client comfort (IPA, 2020). Coaching CPD will likely follow suit, with virtual delivery becoming a formal and essential part of future training and accreditation frameworks.

Viewed together, these five trends reveal how the pandemic did more than disrupt, it expanded what executive coaching could be. It deepened client agendas, possibly renewed trust in coaching as a profession, created new entry points through pro-bono work, accelerated comfort with technology, and perhaps reignited learning. While many of these will need to be observed and researched in a post-pandemic world, it is true that what began as a crisis response matured into a quiet transformation, positioning coaching not just as a leadership tool but as a resource for navigating complexity and change.

But beyond these visible shifts, another opportunity was emerging. As coaching moved into the digital realm, the screen, often seen as a barrier, also became a window. A window into the raw, unguarded textures of a client's life. Coaches found themselves not in sterile meeting rooms, but looking into kitchens, spare bedrooms, corners carved out of family homes or messy home office setups. These weren't just video calls; they became glimpses into the world behind the person. The next section explores what this new vantage point made possible.

5.3 Exploring New Windows

Section 2.2 highlighted that in understanding how technology is shaping executive coaching, a useful parallel emerges from the world of learning theory. Ertmer and Newby (2016) describe a reciprocal relationship between theory and tools: not only do theories influence how technology is used, but tools themselves can reshape theory. Amongst the three main learning theories in educational psychology—*behaviourism*, *cognitive information processing*, and *constructivism*—the role of technology diverges (Ertmer & Newby, 1993, 2013).

In the first two, technology is typically something to be learned about or from. But in *constructivism*, the prevailing model today, technology becomes something to learn *with*. These new windows, which technology had opened up for coaches, provided exactly the perfect case for an opportunity to *learn with technology*.

Executive coaching, too, leans into a constructivist ethos. It is not about transferring knowledge from coach to client, but about creating meaning together (Critchley, 2010). Coaches often work with senior leaders who already bring a deep well of experience. The coach's role is to hold space for reflection, surface insights, and support new awareness (De Haan, 2011; Feldman, 2001). In this way, coaching is a collaborative act of sense-making, one that aligns closely with constructivist learning, where meaning is built from experience rather than handed down.

As coaching moved online, the screen became more than just a medium, it became a window. Not just into the client's home, but into their context, their day-to-day reality, their unfiltered selves. These virtual glimpses created new shared experiences for coach and client alike. And with each experience came fresh opportunities to reflect, interpret, and co-create meaning in real time.

Sharples et al. (2005) suggest that in a technology-mediated world, context is not a static backdrop, it's a dynamic interaction between people and their environment. Bullen et al. (2011) also support such a contextual view of learning, which is also true for coaching. The digital setting doesn't just host the conversation; it *shapes* it. And in that shaping lies a new frontier for learning—one where technology is not merely a channel, but a partner in the coaching relationship.

In one of our conversations, held during the height of the COVID-19 crisis in the UK, Gloria shared a moment from her coaching practice that captured the new possibilities and ethical sensitivities introduced by virtual workspaces. I share that as Case Study 5 below.

Coaching Across Frontlines—Gloria and Her NHS Client (Case Study 5)

Gloria had been supporting frontline staff at the NHS—doctors, nurses, and administrators, many of whom were not only caring for patients with COVID-19 but also their infected colleagues. "That is their environment", she recalled, "and there is me, sitting in the comfort of my own home. I did reference it in terms of that contrast, they're literally on the frontline, and I'm... safe".

The coaching was focused on resilience and coping strategies. But it was the screen itself that introduced something deeper. On one end, Gloria sat in a quiet, rural setting. On the other end, her client joined from a bustling hospital office, often surrounded by background noise, quick interruptions, or the quiet fatigue that follows trauma. It wasn't just words being exchanged, it was context, space, and a visceral difference in reality. The digital window didn't flatten the experience; it enriched it. Gloria became more aware of her own positioning and privilege. Her clients, in turn, often opened up about the emotional load of working in such environments. In one session, the very setting, the beeping of machines in the background, a hurried colleague passing through the frame—became the entry point for a conversation about overwhelm, boundaries, and what "coping" really looked like.

Rather than ignoring the contrast, Gloria acknowledged it. She allowed the screen to become a shared surface for reflection. "It was important not to pretend we were in the same place", she told me. "We weren't. And noticing that made the work more real".

Gloria's case study is a reminder that virtual coaching is not just a workaround, it offers a new window into the lived realities of our clients. When approached with humility and awareness, these windows invite us to deepen the conversation, honour the context, and meet the client not just where they are emotionally, but where they actually live and work.

This opening of the virtual window into newer spaces proved helpful for other coaches as well. Brian started to notice how much more of the client's lived environment was becoming visible, unfiltered, unpolished, and often unspoken. Rather than distractions, these glimpses became meaningful entry points. As Brian noted, "I just look at everything as data".

Peeking into Client's Context—Brian and His Rebel Client (Case Study 6)

Brian recounted an early session with a new client, conducted over video during the pandemic. "He was sitting on his bed", Brian recalled, "the room a bit of a mess". Almost immediately, the client acknowledged it, apologising for the state of his surroundings.

For Brian, it wasn't the mess that mattered, it was the moment. "It was one of the first things he said", he shared, "and not that it bothered me, but it told me something. I just look at everything as data".

That small admission, born out of self-consciousness, sparked a deeper conversation. The client described himself as "a bit of a rebel", someone who resisted structure and often found himself pushing against systems, including organisational norms. What might have passed unnoticed in a traditional office setting, tidy desk, crisp shirt, curated calm, now revealed itself through an unmade bed and a casual demeanour.

The space spoke. And Brian listened.

This wasn't about judgment; it was about expanding the field of awareness. The screen had become more than a medium, it was a lens. Brian used the client's setting as a conversational bridge, inviting reflection on how this self-perception as a "rebel" showed up in work, in relationships, and in leadership choices.

These coaching stories remind us that technology, when used with intention, can deepen presence rather than dilute it. The virtual shift brought more than logistical change, it offered a fresh lens into clients' lived realities. For coaches like Gloria and Brian, the mess, the noise, the interruptions became not distractions but doorways. The screen, once seen as a barrier, turned into a window of insight, intimacy, and shared context. Executive coaching found new ground, not by resisting the medium, but by learning with it.

Yet, as one window opened, another question began to surface. The same digital tide that brought coaches closer to their clients also stirred a quiet unease. What happens when technology doesn't just support coaching, but creates anxiety? In the next chapter, we gently step into this evolving conversation: exploring the rise of digital tools, a bit about AI, the questions it raises about human relevance, and what it means to coach in a world where the tools are becoming more intelligent. It's a chapter about uncertainty, but also one about possibility.

Reflective Exercise 5.1 Thinking About the Pandemic Impact

Looking through the pandemic lens, answer the following questions:

1. How has your coaching practice changed since the pandemic, both in structure and in spirit?
2. Have your clients' coaching agendas shifted in noticeable ways post-pandemic? If so, how have you adapted?
3. How has your own CPD been shaped by the pandemic years? What new capabilities do you now consider essential?
4. What has your relationship with technology become: a reluctant necessity, or an evolving partnership?

Reflective Exercise 5.2 Timeline of Transformation

Trace how your coaching identity evolved during and after the pandemic. **Instructions**: Draw a simple timeline, beginning with March 2020 and ending with the present. Mark 3–5 key turning points in your coaching practice during this period (e.g., first full-virtual client, introduction of a new tool, shift in client agendas). For each turning point, briefly note:

1. What changed in your context?
2. What did you resist?
3. What did you embrace?
4. What did you learn about yourself as a coach?

Use this timeline to surface patterns and notice what has endured vs. what has evolved.

Reflective Exercise 5.3 Take a Pause: Looking Through the Digital Window

Before your next coaching session, take a moment to sit in your coaching space and look around, what does your environment say about you? Then, in the next few sessions, pay quite attention to your client's space. Without judgment or assumption, simply observe. What do you notice that you wouldn't in a face-to-face setting? A background object? A tone in the room? A rhythm of interruptions?

Now reflect on the following questions:

- How might these contextual clues offer a richer understanding of your client's world?
- How can you use this awareness to deepen presence without becoming intrusive?
- When does noticing become data, and when does it become a distraction?

References

Bajpai, B., & Clutterbuck, D. (2024). One-to-one digital coaching. In J. Passmore, S. J. Diller, S. Isaacson, & M. Brantl (Eds.), *The digital and AI coaches' handbook* (pp. 303–312). Routledge.

Berry, R. M. (2005). *A comparison of face-to-face and distance coaching practices: The role of the working alliance in problem resolution*. Georgia State University.

Boyce, L. A., & Clutterbuck, D. (2010). E-coaching: Accept it, it's here, and it's evolving! In L. A. Boyce & D. Clutterbuck (Eds.), *Advancing executive coaching: Setting the course for successful leadership coaching* (pp. 285–315). Jossey-Bass.

Bullen, M., Morgan, T., & Qayyum, A. (2011). Digital learners in higher eduvcation: Generation is not the issue. *Canadian Journal of Learning and Technology/La revue canadienne de l'apprentissage et de la technologie, 37*(1). https://doi.org/10.21432/T2NC7B.

Critchley, B. (2010). Relational coaching: Taking the coaching high road. *Journal of Management Development*, 29(10), 851–863.

De Haan, E. (2011). *Relational coaching: Journeys towards mastering one-to-one learning*. John Wiley & Sons.

Doolittle, J. S. (2022). Virtual coaching is inevitable and effective. *Regent Research Roundtables Proceedings*, 24–31. https://cdn.regent.edu/wp-content/uploads/2022/10/Regent-Research-Roundtables-2022-Professional-Coaching-Doolittle.pdf.

Drucker, P. F. (1993). *The ecological vision: Reflections on the American condition*. Transaction Publishers.

Ertmer, P. A., & Newby, T. J. (1993). Behaviorism, cognitivism, constructivism: Comparing critical features from an instructional design perspective. *Performance Improvement Quarterly*, 6(4), 50–72.

Ertmer, P. A., & Newby, T. J. (2013). Behaviorism, cognitivism, constructivism: Comparing critical features from an instructional design perspective. *Performance Improvement Quarterly*, 26(2), 43–71.

Ertmer, P. A., & Newby, T. J. (2016). Learning theory and technology. A reciprocal relationship. In D. S. N. Rushby (Ed.), *The Wiley handbook of learning technology*. John Wiley & Sons.

Feldman, D. C. (2001). Career coaching: What HR professionals and managers need to know. *Human Resource Planning*, 24(2), 26–35.

Frazee, R. V. (2008). *E-coaching in organizations: A study of features, practices, and determinants of use*. University of San Diego.

Geissler, H., Hasenbein, M., Kanatouri, S., & Wegener, R. (2014). E-coaching: Conceptual and empirical findings of a virtual coaching programme. *International Journal of Evidence Based Coaching and Mentoring*, 12(2), 165.

Ghods, N., & Boyce, C. (2013). Virtual coaching and mentoring. In J. Passmore, D. B. Peterson, & T. Freire (Eds.), *The Wiley-Blackwell handbook of the psychology of coaching and mentoring* (pp. 501–523). Wiley-Blackwell.

Grant, A. (2020, June 1). Adam Grant on how jobs, bosses and firms may improve after the crisis. *Economist*.

Grant, A. M. (2005). What is evidence-based executive, workplace and life coaching? In D. R. Stober & A. M. Grant (Eds.), *Evidence-based coaching handbook: Putting best practices to work for your clients* (pp. 1–12). Wiley.

Grant, A. M. (2006). A personal perspective on professional coaching and the development of coaching psychology. *International Coaching Psychology Review, 1*(1), 12–22.

ICF. (2020). *COVID-19 and the coaching industry*. https://coachingfederation.org/wp-content/uploads/2020/09/FINAL_ICF_GCS2020_COVIDStudy.pdf.

IPA. (2020). Recommendations for psychoanalysts regarding the use of video-conferencing in their practice. www.ipa.world/IPA/en/News/corona_remote_sessions.aspx.

Jarosz, J. (2021). The impact of coaching on well-being and performance of managers and their teams during pandemic. *International Journal of Evidence Based Coaching and Mentoring*, *19*(1), 4–27.

Kanatouri, S. (2020). Digital coaching: A conceptually distinct form of coaching? In S. Greif, H. Möller, & W. Scholl (Eds.), *Coaching im Kontext des digitalen Wandels* (pp. 11–28). Vandenhoeck & Ruprecht.

Kanatouri, S., & Geissler, H. (2017). Adapting to working with new technologies. In T. Bachkirova, G. Spence, & D. Drake (Eds.), *The Sage handbook of coaching* (pp. 715–730). Sage.

Labs, O. (Producer). (2019). The state of remote work report. www.owllabs.com/state-of-remote-work.

Lancaster, S., & Smith, D. (2002). What's in a name? The identity of clinical psychology as a specialty. *Australian Psychologist*, *37*(1), 48–51.

Michalik, N. M., & Schermuly, C. C. (2024). Online, offline, or both? The importance of coaching format for side effects in business coaching. *Journal of Managerial Psychology*, *39*(6), 775–794.

Nicholas, T. (Producer). (2017, December 13). The death of expertise. *The Fedralist*. http://thefederalist.com/2014/01/17/the-death-of-expertise/#.WMxRDDBsakI.twitter

Palmer, S., Panchal, S., & O'Riordan, S. (2020). Could the experience of the COVID-19 pandemic have any positive impact on wellbeing? *European Journal of Applied Positive Psychology*, *4*(10), 2397–7116.

Pascal, A., Sass, M., & Gregory, J. B. (2015). I'm only human: The role of technology in coaching. *Consulting Psychology Journal: Practice and Research*, *67*(2), 100.

Passmore, J., Diller, S. J., Isaacson, S., & Brantl, M. (2024). *The digital and AI coaches' handbook: The complete guide to the use of online, AI, and technology in coaching*. Taylor & Francis.

Politico (Producer). (2020, 6 June 2020). Coronavirus will change the world permanently. Here's how. www.politico.com/news/magazine/2020/03/19/coronavirus-effect-economy-life-society-analysis-covid-135579.

Richard, J. T. (1999). Multimodal therapy: A useful model for the executive coach. *Consulting Psychology Journal: Practice and Research*, *51*(1), 24.

Rossett, A., & Marino, G. (2005). If coaching is good, then e-coaching is. *T AND D*, *59*(11), 46.

Schermuly, C. C., Graßmann, C., Ackermann, S., & Wegener, R. (2022). The future of workplace coaching—An explorative Delphi study. *Coaching: An International Journal of Theory, Research and Practice*, *15*(2), 244–263.

Sharples, M., Taylor, J., & Vavoula, G. (2005). Towards a theory of mobile learning. In H. van der Merwe & T. Brown (Eds.), *Proceedings of mLearn 2005: 4th World Conference on Mobile Learning* (pp. 1–9).

Sherpa Coaching. (2015). *The tenth annual executive coaching survey*. Sherpa Coaching.

Tavis, A., & Woodward, W. (2024). *The digital coaching revolution: How to support employee development with coaching tech*. Kogan Page Publishers.

Virtual Executive Coaching. (2025, January 5). *Skills to lead remotely*. https://tandemcoach.co/virtual-executive-coaching.

6 Paradox of Relevance and Artificial Intelligence

In exploring the question **How are executive coaches engaging with the changes arising out of digitalisation?**, the previous chapters examined how coaches are "encountering" and "experiencing" change—specifically in relation to virtual coaching. Through research insights and literary reflections, we now have a clearer sense of how executive coaches are *responding*, both specifically to the digital shift of virtual coaching, brought on by the pandemic, and more broadly to the evolving technological landscape. With this foundation in place, we now turn to the next layer of inquiry: what are executive coaches "feeling" in response to these changes?

This chapter also includes an introduction to these *feelings* specific to the context of artificial intelligence (AI) tools. It's important to note that the pace of development in this space (of AI) has been extraordinary. My research was completed by October 2022, just a month before the public launch of ChatGPT which dramatically altered the landscape (Teubner et al., 2023). Given this timing, the section on AI research is intentionally concise. It does include some broad contours of what my research unearthed, particularly the framing of AI Optimists vs. AI Critical. The afterword at the end of this book acknowledges the limitations of the book itself, arising from the particular time and context in which this work was undertaken.

The reason I make this reference to the afterword and to the limitations at this stage is to help set readers' expectations when approaching a chapter that has AI in its title. This chapter does not hope to account for the latest developments in AI research, nor is it an attempt to track the fast-evolving implications of conversational AI for executive coaching. These are areas that are changing at such speed that any effort to capture them within a book, where the journey from writing to publication itself spans many months, would risk becoming outdated almost as soon as it is printed.

DOI: 10.4324/9781003638834-9

Having signposted these boundaries, it is important to emphasise that the themes, emotions, and questions surfaced by my respondents remain highly pertinent. Even three years on, what this chapter captures continues to resonate, not because it predicts specific technological trajectories, but because it reveals enduring human concerns. The narratives that emerged from the research echo with striking familiarity in contemporary conversations about AI and coaching, suggesting that while technologies evolve rapidly, the deeper questions of relevance, identity, and meaning unfold at a much slower pace.

6.1 Imagined Irrelevance

One of the more surprising findings of my research was the depth of anxiety executive coaches felt, not just about change, but about their very relevance. I had expected some degree of hesitation, perhaps even discomfort, in the face of rapid digitalisation. After all, the pace of change has been relentless and unsettling for many. But what I hadn't anticipated was the extent to which some coaches were beginning to question their place in the evolving landscape. Not just *how* they coach, but *whether* they would still be needed. Gloria captured this sentiment with striking clarity when she said, "When you strip everything, it boils down to the fear of getting irrelevant". With over 15 years of experience in executive coaching, leadership development, and facilitation, Gloria's words helped crystallise a feeling I had sensed but not yet fully understood. What she named, I describe here as a kind of *imagined irrelevance*, a psychological state where the fear of obsolescence feels real, even if not yet actual.

It's worth noting that this fear was rarely stated directly. None of the coaches I interviewed openly said, "I fear becoming irrelevant". Instead, these emotions surfaced through more subtle cues, half-laughs, offhand remarks, reflections about clients, or throwaway comments that belied something deeper. In fact, several coaches projected the fear onto their clients. One spoke of how their clients often felt "no longer relevant… they carry an existential fear". But the coach didn't immediately extend that thought inward, even though, in the flow of conversation, the line between client and coach was often blurry.

The language that did emerge, words like *fear*, *dread*, *irrelevance*, and *obsolescence*, was unmistakably heavy. And the tone, more often than not, was subdued. Except for a few who were more optimistic, the general outlook on digital tools, coach-tech, and especially AI, was marked by unease. These weren't just professional concerns; they were deeply personal. The fear wasn't simply about falling behind, it was about no longer being seen, no longer mattering. This imagined irrelevance, though not always voiced plainly, sits quietly in the background of many conversations about technology and coaching. And it deserves our attention, not to amplify the fear, but to understand the roots of what one of the coaches had termed as "existential fear", though for his client.

Like him, many other respondents also projected fears of change and obsolescence onto their clients. It was far more common to hear coaches talk about the "existential dread" faced by leaders they worked with than to hear them speak of their own. Turning the spotlight inward seemed harder, perhaps even uncomfortable. Yet there were exceptions. Daniel, for instance, offered a rare and deeply thoughtful reflection. As he explored his client's anxiety about becoming outdated in a fast-changing organisation, he began to draw quiet parallels to his own profession. The way he articulated this connection, without defensiveness, and with a sense of openness, stood out in the interviews.

His story is not just about the client's fears, but about the mirror it held up to the coach himself. Daniel's case, which I discuss next, is a powerful reminder that coaches, too, are navigating the same questions they help their clients confront. And that, within the space of coaching, sometimes the hardest work is not helping others see clearly—but allowing ourselves to do the same.

Daniel—Turkeys Celebrating Christmas (Case Study 7)

Daniel shared a coaching engagement that began as a conversation about leadership but soon turned into something much more layered. His client, a senior professional working in the credit risk function of a financial services firm, had been tasked with developing an AI algorithm to improve decision-making accuracy and speed in credit assessments.

At first, it seemed like a straightforward innovation brief. But as the client began to unpack the assignment, a deeper tension surfaced, one that was hard to ignore. The more effective the algorithm became, the more likely it was that the credit risk team itself would become obsolete. Daniel described the moment vividly, and I share his quote:

"He said to me—'It's like... we have a whole department looking after credit risk, and now I'm building something that questions whether we even need them anymore. I mean, you still need someone to build the algorithm... maybe even include the credit risk experts in doing so—but that just makes them redundant in the long run. It's like turkeys celebrating Christmas'".

It was a sharp metaphor, uncomfortable, even humorous, but loaded with truth. What Daniel's client was expressing was not just a professional dilemma, but a human one. How do you contribute to something that might erase the very ground you, and others like you, stand on? For Daniel, this wasn't just a window into the client's world. It prompted a deeper reflection on his own profession. He wondered aloud if executive coaches themselves weren't in a similar position, supporting clients to embrace digital transformation, while often avoiding those same conversations in their own backyard.

Daniel didn't frame his insight as criticism. It was more of a caution. He believed that large-scale disruptions in the coaching field, especially those driven by AI, would not likely come from within the profession.

"It's hard to expect turkeys to look forward to Christmas", he said with a quiet laugh.

His reflection speaks to a larger theme discussed in this chapter: that "imagined irrelevance" is not just fear, it can also lead to inertia. And if coaches are to remain relevant, not just in their clients' eyes but in their own, they may need to reckon with the same forces of change they so often help others face.

Interestingly, not all coaches agreed with Daniel's perspective. Some felt that, having witnessed their clients grapple with digital disruption, job losses, and obsolescence within their own organisations, many executive coaches were already attuned to the potential upheaval in their own field, and would likely become active partners in shaping that change. Garima even suggested that recent technological advances may be ushering in an era of "enlightened self-interest" amongst the coaching community.

While I'm not entirely sure we can go that far and attribute such a shift solely to digital progress, one thing is clear: the easy availability of online learning resources, often free, has created unprecedented opportunities for self-directed development. It raises an interesting question: how are executive coaches engaging with these resources? Are they using them to play, explore, and grow? And if clients are indeed becoming more self-driven in their development, inspired by this new landscape of access and autonomy, what role will the coach play? Perhaps the coaching relationship will evolve, less about guiding or providing information, and more about holding space, inviting challenge, and deepening reflection. If so, this shift may not signal irrelevance, but rather a reframing of what relevance looks like.

Several respondents resonated with this reframing. Many acknowledged that certain aspects of coaching might lose relevance, given the abundance of digital resources now easily accessible to clients. However, there was little consensus on which aspects those might be. Some pointed to emerging technologies, like virtual reality and artificial intelligence, as having the potential to replace not just parts of coaching, but possibly entire coaching engagements. Willow voiced this possibility candidly: "in some parts of the coaching business use [of] coaches might disappear altogether because you can get so much virtual reality videos, stuff like that. Do you actually need... [what] coaching gives? ... It wouldn't take too much more development for someone to come up with a simulation with an avatar who would actually play a role... You could do it with coaching".

It was certainly an extreme view, but it offered a valuable glimpse into the mental struggle many coaches are navigating. A few senior coaches admitted they might be approaching retirement before such drastic disruptions take hold. Others simply "hoped" the changes would be gradual allowing their current practices to remain relevant. In these conversations, I heard echoes of denial, bargaining, and acceptance (Kubler-Ross, 1969)leading me to wonder: what is the sense of loss beneath these emotional responses?

Perhaps it is the fear of becoming irrelevant, or more subtly, a feeling of *imagined irrelevance*. While most of these discussions were framed around digitalisation and virtual coaching, in the overall context of indirect or direct impact (Figure 3.1), the subject of AI did come up repeatedly. And it is to this theme we now turn: the growing tension between those executive coaches who view AI very critically and others who see its promise with optimism.

6.2 AI Optimists vs. AI Critical

AI is among the most rapidly advancing domains within digitalisation today. Often described as a general-purpose technology, AI is expected to impact nearly every aspect of our economy and daily life. Google's CEO, Sundar Pichai, went so far as to call its impact "more profound than fire and electricity" (Economist, 2020). Over the past decade, the combination of cheaper computing power and growing data availability has accelerated AI's progress. Many of us already interact with AI daily, unlocking phones with facial recognition, receiving predictive text in emails, or using grammar suggestions in documents, often without realising it.

While the "artificial" in AI is broadly understood (non-human, non-biological, and typically digital) and agreed, it is the term "intelligence" that remains contested. One very useful definition comes from Kaplan and Haenlein (2019, p. 17): "Artificial intelligence (AI) is defined as a system's ability to interpret external data correctly, to learn from such data, and to use those learnings to achieve specific goals and tasks through flexible adaptation".

AI is being researched in the areas of *education* (Popenici & Kerr, 2017; Zawacki-Richter et al., 2019), *training* (Tkachenko et al., 2019), and *mental health* (Luxton, 2016). By 2022, adjacent areas of coaching like *health coaching* (Sqalli & Al-Thani, 2019), *fitness coaching* (Stein & Brooks, 2017), and *sports coaching* (Claudino et al., 2019) were starting to see some research on AI, but the agenda had not yet found momentum in the field of executive coaching. This has changed since. While not specifically developed for executive coaching, the definition by Kaplan and Haenlein is helpful. What makes this definition helpful for coaching is its emphasis on *learning* and *flexible adaptation*, qualities we often associate with effective coaching conversations. Just as a coach listens, reflects, and adjusts in real time, an AI system built on large datasets can theoretically do the same: recognise patterns in a client's language, adjust responses based on prior input, and guide the client towards clarity or insight. This conceptual overlap, between adaptive systems and responsive coaching, opens the door to a provocative possibility: if AI can learn to interpret data, adjust flexibly, and ask context-sensitive questions, could it then function as a coach?

Rohan, a veteran coach with over 30 years of experience, now running his own leadership advisory and supervision practice in India, expressed a clear belief: AI coaches were not just possible, they were imminent. "It is not difficult to visualise a situation where an AI-powered interface will replace executive coaches", he said. His conviction was echoed by Nikhil, another experienced Indian coach with a background in organisational consulting. Nikhil shared that a few client organisations had approached him with serious interest in developing AI-based coaching tools. One of them, he recounted, proposed: "Give 100,000 hours of the best coaching, and I'll create a language-sensitive coach for you". He was not alone. Prakash, also an executive coach and HR consultant, had heard a similar proposition from a close associate working in natural language processing. Prakash recalled his friend saying, "Give me a thousand hours of coaching conversations by great coaches, and I'll build you a coaching bot".

I refer to respondents like Rohan, Nikhil, and Prakash as **AI Optimists**. For them, the idea of an AI-powered coach is not science fiction, it's a logical next step, especially given the rapid strides in machine learning and natural language understanding. Even Brian, who doesn't identify as an AI Optimist, acknowledged the trend: "There are people busy trying to create sort of machine coaching bots". Prakash championed the idea further to suggest that "with machine learning, there is absolutely no reason why you should not be able to build a coach bot; what is a coach doing? We pride ourselves on saying that we don't give answers. We ask the right questions".

Some of this optimism stems from the rapid progress in machine learning and a belief that artificial general intelligence (AGI) might be just around the corner. Popular imagination often anthropomorphises AI, envisioning talking machines and autonomous robots. However, the actual development of AGI, the kind required for such science-fiction scenarios (Taulli & Oni, 2019), has been far slower. The fact that, even after a decade of hype and billions in investment, we still don't see fully autonomous vehicles on our roads (especially outside the US) is a telling example. While AI will undoubtedly continue advancing in pattern recognition and task-specific domains (known as Narrow or Weak AI), it remains unlikely that we will see the emergence of Strong AI, the kind capable of human-level general intelligence, anytime soon.

Underlying the views of AI Optimists was also a common assumption about coaching: that the essence of coaching lies in detecting patterns and asking the right questions. Since coaches often pride themselves on not giving answers but guiding reflection, these respondents believed this function could be replicated by AI. Their reasoning was simple, if large volumes of high-quality coaching conversations could be fed into a learning model, then with enough training, an AI system could be capable of posing insightful, even transformative questions. For the AI Optimists, the question was no longer whether AI could play a coaching role, but how soon it would.

At this point, we must pause and ask, **is the essence of coaching really just about asking questions?** Many respondents challenged this idea. Eshwar, for instance, raised a series of reflections in his typically thoughtful style: "Suppose I say, 'Alexa, I think I have a problem, … Can you coach me?' I don't know. Will Alexa work with my voice? Will it work with my situation? Will it work with the way I have framed the issue? Will it reframe that issue and help me reframe it? Will it ask me the questions that would be of help to me? What extent of my context would be important? It raises many questions".

Eshwar's questions expose the complexity hidden within what may seem like a simple coaching move, asking a question. Even if one accepts (only for argument's sake) that a coach's primary role is to ask the right questions, many subtle factors still come into play: tone, timing, framing, reframing, and above all, context. These dimensions, so often invisible, matter deeply in a human interaction. Other AI-Optimist respondents acknowledged that with enough data, an AI might eventually ask good questions in certain situations. But some also questioned whether asking the "right question" is the whole story. Several felt that this ability, while essential, is only one small piece of a much larger human process.

Daniel articulated it well: "The act of saying it to someone and it being heard is very different from it being said to a bot or an algorithm, even if the algorithm or the bot comes back with a technically better question". For him, the power of coaching lies not just in the question itself, but in the **experience of being heard by another human being.** Without that, something vital gets lost. These voices belonged to the second category of executive coaches, whom I refer to as **AI Critical.**

The AI Critical position challenges the notion of AI as a viable replacement for executive coaches, either dismissing it altogether or acknowledging only a narrow, supporting role in certain contexts. Gloria, a strong champion of the AI Critical camp, made a deeply humanistic case, suggesting that what lies at the heart of coaching cannot be programmed. "Could you build into a machine actually that **desire to help another human** being because that's what I sit there with", she said. For her, coaching begins not with data, but with intention, with a desire to be of service to another person.

This emphasis on human qualities—desire, care, presence—is central to the AI Critical view. Coaches like Garima and Gloria questioned not just what AI can do, but what it cannot *feel*. "See, I think what the AI coach will not be able to do is care", Garima said simply. Gloria added, "It's about empathy, isn't it? That's at the heart of coaching. Can artificial intelligence demonstrate empathy?" Their concerns go beyond technical capacity. They touch on the very soul of coaching as a human relationship, one built not only on asking questions but on *being with* the client in moments of uncertainty, insight, and vulnerability. While AI might replicate surface-level behaviours, posing reflective questions, offering frameworks, tracking goals, it cannot (yet) simulate the depth of human connection that many coaches believe is essential to meaningful change.

Interestingly, while both Gloria and Garima took an overall AI Critical stance, they also, at different points in their interviews, acknowledged the potential threat posed by AI coaches. There was a quiet uncertainty that lingered beneath their convictions, a recognition that, despite current limitations, AI might eventually bridge some of these gaps. Grace introduced an important nuance in this debate: the difference between *having* empathy and *demonstrating* it. She pointed out that AI systems, by selecting the right words, tone, and phrasing, could create an *appearance* of empathy, enough, perhaps, for clients to feel emotionally held, even if that care is not authentically present in the system itself.

As one coach put it, "To replicate the actual felt and human experience of being in a relationship… who knows? I dread to think. I hope that it's not possible". This hesitation reveals a deeper anxiety, not just about what AI can *do*, but about what clients might come to *accept*. If a convincing simulation of care is enough to sustain a coaching relationship, what becomes of the role of real human connection? This subtle tension, between believing in the irreplaceable value of human presence, and fearing that AI might still imitate it well enough, was expressed by many coaches who took an overall AI Critical position.

In summary, the findings indicate that most executive coaches believed an AI coach was unlikely to replace a real coach anytime soon, largely because of AI's current inability to experience authentic human emotions or offer genuine empathy. Yet, these same coaches expressed unease at the possibility that AI might someday in the future *replicate* such emotional presence convincingly enough to be useful to clients.

While they did not perceive an immediate existential threat, a quiet disquiet persisted. After years of training, practice, and professional investment, they worried, however faintly, that it could all be upended by rapid technological advances. As Gloria reflected, "My question I'm posing is—do you need to have a decade plus of building up coaching experience and then immersing yourself in a profession to be effective? Or could actually an algorithm perhaps be even more effective than a human being can be at identifying what an issue is, offering up insights?" Her question captures the tension that many AI Critical respondents wrestled with.

None of the executive coaches I spoke with had any deep technical knowledge of AI, and their concerns were rarely based on a first-hand understanding of machine learning or natural language processing. Instead, their sense of imagined irrelevance, and the dread it carried, stemmed more from possibility than probability. Some named their fears openly. Others circled them indirectly. But beneath the varied expressions lay a shared discomfort, one that extended beyond AI. It was not just the potential of being replaced that unsettled them. Perhaps their deeper fear stemmed from the sheer speed and scale of the technological transformation unfolding around them. This brings us to the next emotional undercurrent that surfaced in my research, this wasn't specific to AI, but anchored to change.

6.3 Fearing Change

As one coach put it, "This pace of change is something we, as a species, have never experienced before". The scale and speed of technological transformation, already discussed in Part 1 of this book, set a great backdrop for what emerged in the findings: executive coaches, like other stakeholders, were feeling unsettled by the digital shift. They weren't just curious or cautious, they were, in many cases, also fearful.

While reading the previous line, it's worth caveating that my data collection took place against the backdrop of the COVID-19 pandemic, a time when the entire world was grappling with uncertainty and anxiety. In that sense, the fear expressed by coaches might well have been part of a broader human response to disruption. I do not claim to separate pandemic-related unease from digital change-related fear; the two were too closely intertwined to be clearly distinguished. Yet, a few respondents did explicitly name the source of their discomfort, not referring to the pandemic, but anchoring it to the velocity of change. It is by focusing on these voices that the next theme emerged: the fear of change itself.

Findings suggest that the fear of change among executive coaches was driven less by their ability to adapt and more by the uncertainty of what coaching in the digital age might come to mean. Ganga captured this nuance when she reflected, "...there may be more fear... because things are so much more uncertain". Many respondents echoed her sentiment. Like most people, executive coaches seemed to long for some sense of certainty, and in a context where familiar ways of working were rapidly shifting, that sense felt increasingly out of reach. Some of this uncertainty stemmed from a lack of training. None of the coaches I interviewed had received professional training or participated in continuous professional development (CPD) that addressed digital tools or the broader technological agenda in coaching. One coach summed up this lack of training quite vividly: "So where do I look? [during my video coaching session] There's this light at the top of the screen, there's the camera, and then the eyes of the client, I feel uncertain and unsure".

It was a small detail, but a telling one. Many of these executive coaches had trained in a time when face-to-face coaching was the norm and digital tools were barely part of the conversation. Eye contact, presence, relational depth, these were once embodied, physical experiences. Few had ever practised creating connection through a screen, and even fewer had been taught how. Faced with a growing array of video conferencing platforms and remote formats, several respondents expressed a clear desire for support, whether through CPD, peer learning, or supervision, to help them navigate this transition. Their fear, it seemed, was not just about technology, but about feeling left to figure it out alone.

In parallel to their frustration with the lack of available support, many respondents acknowledged the challenges of learning new skills and factors that might impact executive coaches' ability to change and be ready for the digital age. Two factors—age and attitude, emerged as possible barriers to such change.

Several respondents noted that the relatively older age profile of many executive coaches may make it harder for some to keep pace with rapid technological advances and digital disruptions. Brian (aged 60–65) openly shared that he felt too old to adapt. He hoped there would still be enough demand for face-to-face coaching after the pandemic, as he had little desire to move his practice online. Anil (aged 70–75), one of the most senior coaches I interviewed, was more forthright. He dismissed digital platforms as "new age games" more suitable for "younger coaches like you", he put it. Gloria added perspective from her experience on virtual coaching forums: "but coaches tend to be older. And I've been on a lot of community coaching calls, and some people are really struggling with the technology and probably not even really struggling with it. They're just struggling with the thought of the technology rather than probably the actual reality…".

Taken together, these voices suggest that age may influence a coach's ease with digital change. But equating age with resistance would be an oversimplification. One of the oldest coaches I interviewed, Rohan (aged 70–75), was one of the most digitally curious and future-focused. He was actively engaging with coach-tech, knew multiple digital platforms in depth, and had already been experimenting with virtual CPD formats in his organisation. In contrast, Leah (aged 45–50), one of the younger respondents, showed little interest in digital coaching developments and was a reluctant user of virtual tools. Her case, along with Rohan's, reminds us that openness to change is shaped as much by attitude as by age.

Research echoes this interplay between age and attitude. Scholars like Prensky (2010) and Howlett and Waemusa (2018) have explored the connection between age and confidence in technology use by contrasting digital immigrants and digital natives. However, not all research supports such a strict generational divide. Bullen et al. (2011), for instance, challenge the notion that age alone determines tech affinity. Their work suggests—and my findings confirm, that attitude plays an equally, if not more, significant role. Executive coaches who showed curiosity, openness, or had prior engagement with digital tools appeared far less apprehensive about coaching in the digital age than those who were more resistant or disengaged. This pattern also aligns well with findings from HAI research (Fenichel, 2011; von der Pütten et al., 2010) where scholars highlight how personality traits and openness to technology shape one's comfort with digital tools.

In essence, it may not be the year of birth that matters, but the mindset and attitude with which coaches approach change. My findings support the view that it is not age alone, but more likely the coach's personality that shapes their response to digital change. Specifically, an executive coach's affinity for, or aversion to, technology-driven transformation often appeared to influence how they engaged with it. Willow offered a telling example from her own organisation, where three executive coaches had responded differently to the shift to virtual formats. She observed that her colleagues, both more introverted by nature, seemed quite at ease in the virtual environment, while she, an extrovert, found herself longing for face-to-face interaction. Her reflection introduces the idea that personality traits, along with underlying attitudes, are important factors in how coaches experience and navigate the digital age.

Apart from the two factors of age and attitude (or personality), several respondents suggested that digital change is also likely to impact certain kinds of coaching work more than others. This insight had little to do with the coach as a person and more to do with the nature and quality of the coaching they offered. It was not about the label coaches used to describe their practice, but about how they coached.

Many respondents believed that formulaic coaching, or in Rohan's words, "coaches who operated like a robot", would be particularly vulnerable to replacement by digital or AI-based systems. This discussion reminded me of one of my favourite phrases, which I often use when talking about digital tools and the rise of AI bots: "A bot is unlikely to replace you as a coach, but if you coach like a bot, it is quite likely you will be replaced". Let me pause briefly here and expand on that thought before returning to the respondents' views.

Like most people learning a new skill or craft, many executive coaches begin their journey by being trained in a particular approach or framework. This has given rise to a growing list of models and acronyms in the coaching world. A few illustrative examples include the GROW Model (Whitmore, 2002), STEEP Model (Downey, 1999),

SUCCESS Model (Goldsmith & Lyons, 2011), and OSKAR Model (Jackson & McKergow, 2002).

The value of these models, especially early in a coach's development, cannot be overstated. They offer clarity, structure, and a helpful scaffold when coaches are still finding their feet. At a time when many are fuelled by the desire to help but are unsure how, such frameworks serve as reassuring guideposts. In many ways, they are essential tools in a coach's early toolkit.

But like all tools, they come with limitations. And if used rigidly or unreflectively, they can constrain rather than enable. As coaches grow in confidence and deepen their presence, many begin to evolve beyond any one model or technique. Over time, they develop a more fluid and intuitive way of working, a signature style that emerges from experience, presence, and real connection with the client.

This is especially true when working with senior, seasoned executives who are not only familiar with life's complexities but are also quick to sense when a conversation feels scripted or inauthentic. One senior academic client shared a telling comment about a previous coaching experience. He said that "Within the first five minutes, the coach was asking me about my feelings, and then he kept paraphrasing my sentences by using the last few words, what a load of BS. I knew this wasn't going to work". Unsurprisingly, the coach was not used beyond the first session.

This was exactly the kind of coaching Rohan was cautioning against when he spoke of coaches who "operate like robots". It's not that structure is bad or models are unhelpful. It's that when these are applied mechanically, without presence, without adaptation, and without the human element, they start to resemble scripts. And scripts are far easier for machines to master than human beings.

When visualising coaching in the digital age, a senior coach reflected on how one particular end of the coaching spectrum was far more likely to be disrupted than the other. He remarked: "I like to believe that I do something that a machine can't do, but… if I look at the spectrum of coaching, from ontological coaching on the left to maybe results coaching on the right". The research findings support that results coaching, which is based on fixed steps or set processes, is likely to be disrupted quickly. His reflection echoed a broader pattern in the findings: digital setups were seen as more likely to disrupt coaching approaches that relied on steps, structures, or set processes.

While most executive coaches were dismissive of the effectiveness of overly rigid, step-based approaches, especially in the nuanced world of executive coaching, a few did acknowledge that there might still be a role for this kind of coaching in organisational settings. Daniel, for instance, shared an experience that challenged the prevailing assumption. He described a programme where individuals were trained as coaches in a single day. The training focused entirely on a step-by-step framework, and coaches were instructed to follow it exactly, no deviations permitted. To his surprise, the process was still effective. Daniel proposed that his training was "on the GROW model, [which] lends itself to being automated. We used to do the side of GROW on a program many years ago, where we would just ask the questions, and it works. People are quite astounded".

Daniel's story highlights an important nuance. While highly structured, scripted coaching may not appeal to most experienced executive coaches, or to their senior clients, it might still have its place. In large organisations, where scale, speed, and consistency are often valued, step-based coaching delivered through digital means may offer an efficient solution. The concern, of course, is not whether it works in some contexts, but what might be lost if such methods become the default mode of coaching in the digital age.

In summary, the fear of change observed among executive coaches was not simply a reaction to technology itself, but to the uncertainty, isolation, and loss of familiarity. This fear finds expression in many forms, concerns about skill gaps, anxieties about age or attitude, and discomfort with rigid or formulaic coaching being replaced by automated systems. And yet, even as these fears surface, something coexisted alongside. It was intriguing to discover that many of the same respondents who voiced concerns about becoming obsolete also spoke with conviction about the enduring human aspects of coaching, those they believed no machine could replicate. This simultaneous experience leads us to the concluding section of this chapter.

6.4 Paradox of Obsolescence and Significance

One of the most intriguing findings in this research was the simultaneous presence of two seemingly opposing beliefs among executive coaches: a *fear of obsolescence* and a strong *confidence in their continued significance*. Many respondents, often in the same breath, spoke of the parts of coaching they believed were at risk of being replaced, and the parts they were certain no machine could replicate. What an interesting paradox that is.

To better understand this tension, I revisited the two groups discussed earlier in the chapter: the *AI Optimists* and the *AI Critical*. At first glance, these groups may appear distinct, even polarised. But as I listened more closely, it became evident that they weren't two isolated camps. Rather, they seemed like different vantage points within the same broader landscape, positions that respondents moved between as they made sense of a rapidly changing world. It's entirely possible that these were less fixed identities and more reflective stances adopted in conversation, shaped by the complex and at times contradictory nature of the digital age itself.

So let's briefly look back at the core of their beliefs. The *AI Optimists*, a smaller group, tended to focus on the functional side of coaching. They saw the role of a coach, primarily, as someone who asks powerful questions, a view that does not find strong support in coaching research (De Haan et al., 2020; O'Neill, 2011). From this position, they argued, it was entirely plausible that with enough data, machine learning could eventually generate systems that replicate this questioning process. Some recent studies (Arakawa and Yakura, 2022; Terblanche et al., 2022) suggest that such possibilities are beginning to emerge in structured coaching environments.

In contrast, the *AI Critical* group held a more humanistic view. They believed that AI, regardless of its data-processing power, could never replace the relational depth, emotional intelligence, and caring presence that define impactful coaching. Their objections were based less on technical limitations and more on qualities they saw as uniquely human, empathy, intention, the desire to serve. Interestingly, though, even this group, while sceptical, occasionally wondered whether AI might eventually evolve to simulate care convincingly enough to meet client expectations. Their stance wasn't entirely dismissive, it was cautious, tinged with concern.

What was most revealing, however, was that this paradox didn't map neatly onto the two groups. Being an AI Optimist didn't automatically mean the respondent was free of dread; nor did being AI Critical imply a lack of confidence in human coaching. The relationship was more complex. Some optimists were deeply uneasy about what might be lost; some critics held firm faith in the enduring relevance of human

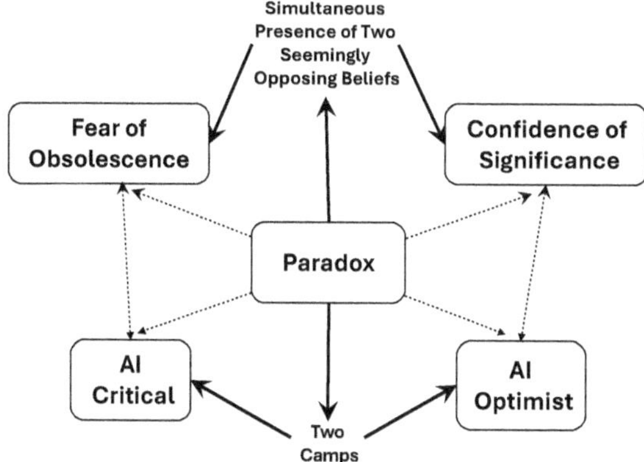

Figure 6.1 Paradox of Obsolescence and Significance

connection. It was less about labels and more about navigating an in-between space, a space where fear and faith coexisted.

To illustrate this, Figure 6.1 summarises the interplay between these perspectives. This figure now offers future researchers a framework to explore this paradox further.

What I can say with clarity from this research is this: most executive coaches felt that formulaic, step-based coaching was vulnerable to automation. In contrast, more relational, reflective, and holistic work—work that required presence, empathy, and trust, was seen as far less likely to be replaced by AI in the near future. And that brings us to the edge of an important shift in our conversation. This paradox, the simultaneous fear of being replaced and confidence in being irreplaceable, mirrors the broader tensions of coaching in the digital age. It is from within this very tension that a new question emerges: *How can executive coaches not only respond to this changing landscape but also prepare to thrive in it?*

That is the focus of **Part 3** of this book.

In the chapters that follow, we shift our gaze forward. We bring together the background landscape of the world and organisations and leaders (Part 1) with the findings of my research (Part 2) and evolve a road ahead for the future. Drawing from the insights uncovered in the earlier chapters, we now explore what it means to be *future-ready* as an executive coach. We look at practical strategies, evolving mindsets, and emerging capabilities that can help coaches stay relevant, effective, and grounded, no matter how fast the world changes.

Reflective Exercise 6.1 Sitting with the Question of Relevance

Before moving to the next chapter, take a moment to turn inward. This chapter explored fears that often stay below the surface, about relevance, change, and what the future might mean for coaching as we know it. The questions below are not for quick answers, but for creating a moment of reflection. They're here to help you notice what's stirring in you, just as you would invite a client to do. Sit with them. See what emerges.

1. What part of my coaching identity feels most challenged by emerging digital or AI tools, and why?
2. Am I more comfortable talking about my client's fears of disruption than exploring my own? What might that say about my relationship to change?
3. In what ways might I be holding on to ways of working that no longer serve the future I want to coach in?
4. What do I believe makes coaching irreplaceable, and is that belief still true in a digitally evolving world?
5. If a disruption were to reshape the coaching profession tomorrow, would I be ready to adapt, or resist? Why?

Reflective Exercise 6.2 Facing the Mirror: Coaching in the Age of AI

This chapter explored a range of responses to the rise of AI, from cautious optimism to quiet dread. Some coaches saw opportunity; others feared obsolescence. And many found themselves somewhere in between, curious but unsure, alert but unprepared. Beneath the surface of technical feasibility lies a deeper inquiry: What does the possibility of AI-powered coaching evoke in us, not just as professionals, but as human beings? These questions invite you to examine your own beliefs, anxieties, and readiness in the face of AI's growing presence in the coaching world.

1. What is your immediate emotional response to the idea of an AI-powered coaching tool? What might that emotion be pointing to?
2. Do you believe that a machine can replicate the essence of coaching? Why or why not?

3. Which aspects of your coaching practice do you consider most irreplaceable, and are those aspects truly beyond the reach of AI?
4. If your clients begin engaging with AI-driven tools for support or insight, how might that impact your sense of professional identity?
5. Are you choosing to stay informed about AI developments in coaching, or choosing to stay away? What might that choice reveal?

References

Arakawa, R., & Yakura, H. (2022) Human–AI communication for human–human communication: Applying interpretable unsupervised anomaly detection to executive coaching. *arXiv preprint arXiv:2206.10987.*

Bullen, M., Morgan, T., & Qayyum, A. (2011). Digital learners in higher education: Generation is not the issue. *Canadian Journal of Learning and Technology/La revue canadienne de l'apprentissage et de la technologie, 37*(1). https://doi.org/10.21432/T2NC7B.

Claudino, J. G., de Oliveira Capanema, D., de Souza, T. V., Serrão, J. C., Pereira, A. C. M., & Nassis, G. P. (2019). Current approaches to the use of artificial intelligence for injury risk assessment and performance prediction in team sports: A systematic review. *Sports Medicine—Open, 5*(1), 28.

De Haan, E., Molyn, J., & Nilsson, V. O. (2020). New findings on the effectiveness of the coaching relationship: Time to think differently about active ingredients? *Consulting Psychology Journal: Practice and Research, 72*(3), 155.

Downey, M. (1999). *Effective coaching.* Orion Business.

Economist. (2020, June 11). An understanding of AI's limitations is starting to sink in. *Economist.*

Fenichel, M. (2011). Online behavior, communication, and experience. In R. Kraus, G. Stricker, & C. Speyer (Eds.), *Online counseling* (pp. 3–20). Elsevier.

Goldsmith, M., & Lyons, L. S. (2011). *Coaching for leadership: The practice of leadership coaching from the world's greatest coaches* (Vol. 152). John Wiley & Sons.

Howlett, G., & Waemusa, Z. (2018). Digital native/digital immigrant divide: EFL teachers' mobile device experiences and practice. *Contemporary Educational Technology, 9*(4), 374–389.

Jackson, P. Z., & McKergow, M. (2002). *Solutions focus.* Nicholas Brealey Publishing.

Kaplan, A., & Haenlein, M. (2019). Siri, Siri, in my hand: Who's the fairest in the land? On the interpretations, illustrations, and implications of artificial intelligence. *Business Horizons, 62*(1), 15–25.

Kubler-Ross, E. (1969). *On death and dying.* Macmillan.

Luxton, D. D. (2016). An introduction to artificial intelligence in behavioral and mental health care. In D. D. Luxton (Ed.), *Artificial intelligence in behavioral and mental health care* (pp. 1–26). Elsevier.

O'Neill, M. B. (2011). *Executive coaching with backbone and heart: A systems approach to engaging leaders with their challenges.* John Wiley & Sons.

Popenici, S. A., & Kerr, S. (2017). Exploring the impact of artificial intelligence on teaching and learning in higher education. *Research and Practice in Technology Enhanced Learning, 12*(1), 22.

Prensky, M. (2010). *Teaching digital natives: Partnering for real learning.* Corwin Press.

Sqalli, M. T., & Al-Thani, D. (2019). AI-supported health coaching model for patients with chronic diseases. In *Proceedings of the 2019 16th International Symposium on Wireless Communication Systems (ISWCS)* (pp. 548–552). IEEE. (Lisbon, Portugal, August 27–30, 2019).

Stein, N., & Brooks, K. (2017). A fully automated conversational artificial intelligence for weight loss: Longitudinal observational study among overweight and obese adults. *JMIR Diabetes*, 2(2), e28.

Taulli, T., & Oni, M. (2019). *Artificial intelligence basics*. Springer.

Terblanche, N., Molyn, J., De Haan, E., & Nilsson, V. O. (2022). Comparing artificial intelligence and human coaching goal attainment efficacy. *PloS One*, *17*(6), e0270255.

Teubner, T., Flath, C. M., Weinhardt, C., Van Der Aalst, W., & Hinz, O. (2023). Welcome to the era of ChatGPT et al. The prospects of large language models. *Business & Information Systems Engineering*, *65*(2), 95–101.

Tkachenko, V., Kuzior, A., & Kwilinski, A. (2019). Introduction of artificial intelligence tools into the training methods of entrepreneurship activities. *Journal of Entrepreneurship Education*, *22*(6), 1–10.

von der Pütten, A. M., Krämer, N. C., & Gratch, J. (2010). How our personality shapes our interactions with virtual characters: Implications for research and development. In J. Allbeck, N. Badler, T. Bickmore, C. Pelachaud, & A. Safonova (Eds.), *Intelligent virtual agents* (Lecture Notes in Computer Science, Vol. 6356, pp. 208–221). Springer.

Whitmore, J. (2002). *Coaching for performance*. Nicholas Brealey Publishing.

Zawacki-Richter, O., Marín, V. I., Bond, M., & Gouverneur, F. (2019). Systematic review of research on artificial intelligence applications in higher education—Where are the educators? *International Journal of Educational Technology in Higher Education*, *16*(1), 39.

Part 3

Reimagining Coaching for a Digital Future

7 The 4-Winged Framework©

Exploring the question *How are executive coaches engaging with the changes arising out of digitalisation?*—we've already travelled a considerable distance together. **Part 1** of this book set the stage and painted the landscape: it detailed the accelerating digital transformation shaping the world we live in, and how executive coaches are called to support the organisations and leaders. We then explored the scope and impact of these shifts and how they are reshaping not just the *what* of coaching, but also the *where*, *how*, and *why*. In **Part 2**, drawing from the findings of my research, we stepped into the lived realities of coaches themselves. We heard their stories, of grappling with change, navigating uncertainty, resisting and adapting, losing footing, and finding new ground. What emerged was not a single narrative, but a rich and layered portrait. Executive coaches today are not merely adjusting to external change, they are moving through a deeper transformation that touches their practice, their relationships, their sense of professional identity, and their inner orientation to the future.

This chapter introduces the **4-Winged Framework©**, a model to make sense of this complex, layered landscape. The framework is grounded in the empirical findings discussed across Chapters 3 to 6, and is best understood when viewed in the background of the broader landscape mapped out in Part 1. It offers a way to integrate what we've learned, both from the world around us and from the lived experiences of coaches, into a cohesive structure.

Given the breadth of research findings, it's understandable if the reader occasionally feels a little adrift. To help navigate the discussions that follow, I've summarised the key themes and sub-themes from the research in Table 7.1. As you move through the rest of the book, you may find it useful to return to this table from time to time to trace connections and locate ideas within the larger narrative. I found it invaluable while shaping Part 3, and I hope it serves you just as well.

DOI: 10.4324/9781003638834-11

Table 7.1 Summary of Part 1 and Part 2

Conceptual Category	*Key Themes*	*Sub Themes*
Chapter 3 **Encountering Change**	• *Experience of Digitalisation* • *Changing Coaching Agenda*	• Digitalisation as Understood by Coaches
		• Direct vs. Indirect Impact of Digitalisation on Executive Coaching
		• Evolving Coaching Agenda
		• Need for Greater Empathy
Chapter 4 **Experiencing Loss of Depth**	• *Blurring of Boundaries* • *Disturbed Presence* • *Absent Physicality*	• No Transition to Coaching Sessions
		• Always Connected Lives of Clients
		• Sense of Disembodiment
		• Fewer Cues—Missing Nuances
		• Weaker Relationships and Working Alliance
		• Inability to Curate and Use the Space
		• Issues of Privacy, Access, and Privilege
Chapter 5 **Opening of New Windows**	• *Benefits of Virtual Coaching* • *Impact of Pandemic*	• Accessibility, Cost-Efficiency, Flexibility, and Reach Across Geographies
		• Inclusion, Scalability, Reduced Environmental Footprint
		• Changing Agendas: Well-Being and Purpose
		• Return of the Expert, Spirit of Service
		• Tech as a Coaching Partner, The CPD Surge
Chapter 6 **Imagining Irrelevance**	• *Paradox of Obsolescence and Significance*	• Simultaneous Dread of Obsolescence and Confidence of Significance
		• Two Camps of AI Critical vs. AI Optimist: Attitude to Tech Adoption
		• Uncertain Future: Lack of Training, CPD, and Supervision
		• AI Might Replace Some Forms of Coaching

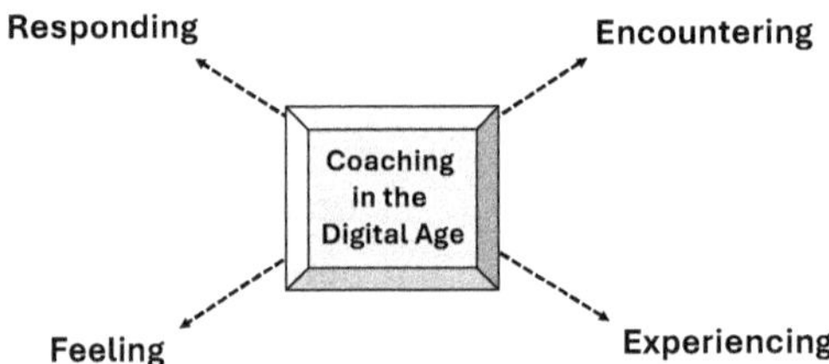

Figure 7.1 Key Dimensions of Coaching in the Digital Age

Before introducing you to the 4-Winged Framework©, I offer a simplified construct built from foundational elements that forms its underlying spine. These foundational elements, illustrated in Figure 7.1, represent the key dimensions of the coaching experience as revealed through this research, they can also serve as a summary of the core findings. As Aguinaldo (2004) reminds us, research findings within a social constructivist paradigm are always partial and situated, given that researchers "actively construct the social world which is itself an interpretation and in need of interpretation" (2004, p. 128). Staying true to constructivist grounded theory, the findings in this book reflect not only the meaning-making of the participants but my own interpretive engagement as a researcher (Bryant, 2002; Charmaz, 2014). Figure 7.1 is one such interpretation. The four elements that follow provide a conceptual bridge into the full framework. They cover:

- How executive coaches **encounter** digital change (Chapter 3)
- How they **experience** a loss of connection and relational depth (Chapter 4)
- How they are **responding**, with experimentation and creativity (Chapter 5)
- How they **feel**, paradoxes of irrelevance and attitude towards AI (Chapter 6)

Taken together, these four elements form a dynamic structure, a living framework. One that can help coaches locate themselves in this shifting terrain, make sense of their current realities, and reflect on the capacities they may need, both inner and outer, for the journey ahead.

Let us now step into the model.

7.1 Introducing the 4-Winged Framework©

Figure 7.2 brings the empirical findings and interpretive analysis together, integrating the four conceptual categories from Table 7.1 and the thematic elements from Figure 7.1 into a single holistic model, the **4-Winged Framework© for Coaching in the Digital Age.**

One note before we begin: the conceptual category originally labelled *Opening of New Windows* has now been expanded and renamed **Navigating the Future.** This change reflects a broader scope. Rather than limiting the discussion to virtual settings and screen-based coaching, this reframing acknowledges the growing ecosystem of digital tools, AI platforms, and tech-enabled coaching environments now shaping the coaching industry. This specific expanded interpretation will be discussed in detail in Chapter 8. For now, let's focus on the framework itself.

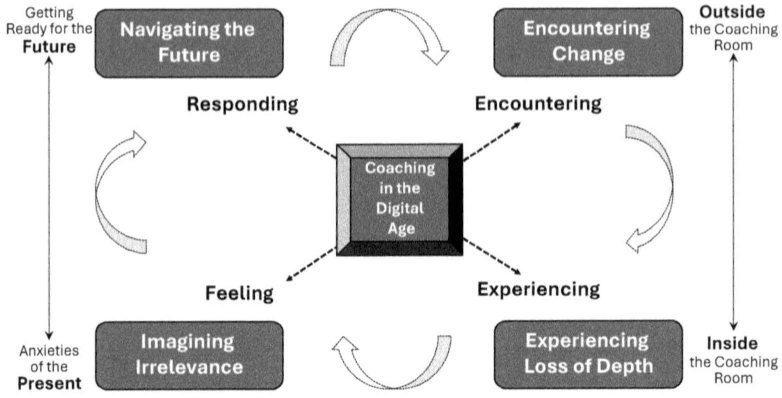

Figure 7.2 4-Winged Framework© for Coaching in the Digital Age

The curved arrows in Figure 7.2 represent one possible path that coaches might follow. In this sequence, they *encounter* digitalisation-led change, *experience* a loss of depth and connection, *feel* a sense of irrelevance or uncertainty, and then *respond* in ways that help them navigate the digital future, before encountering further change again. In other words, the cycle restarts. Of course, this path is not universal. Coaches may enter at different points, follow distinct routes, or bypass some elements entirely. What the **4-Winged Framework©** offers is not a fixed view, but a **language and lens**, a way to understand, articulate, and reflect on the multifaceted impact of digitalisation on executive coaching.

At this juncture, it is also important to emphasise that my research findings are tentative, provisional, and still evolving. They are *tentative* because they do not claim universal truth; rather, they represent one construction of social reality, shaped by the voices of the respondents and interpreted through my lens as a researcher. They are *provisional* in the sense that, like all research, they are bounded by limitations, which I mention later in the book. And they are *developing* because the proposed directions for future research will likely build on, challenge, or refine these findings further.

A rich body of literature exists on the impact of ongoing digitalisation on leaders (Avolio et al., 2014; Cortellazzo et al., 2019; Kane et al., 2019; Khan, 2016; Mohammad, 2009), organisations (Alavi et al., 2014; Colbert et al., 2016; Parviainen et al., 2017; Qiu & Pesch, 2019; Schwab, 2016; Vey et al., 2017), and broader digital transformation trends (Henriette et al., 2016).

However, in sharp contrast, the field of executive coaching remains underexplored in this context. Very little research addresses digitalisation as a socio-contextual movement that holistically affects coaching practice. Even more striking is the near-total absence of scholarship that examines how executive coaches themselves *encounter*, *experience*, *feel*, and *respond* to these changes in an integrated manner. The findings of my research underscore both the significant impact of digitalisation on the work of executive coaches and the challenges they face in making sense of this transformation. What has been missing from the literature is a cohesive, practice-oriented framework that helps coaches understand their own position in this shifting landscape, not only in terms of technique or tools, but at the level of identity, experience, and response. This is precisely the gap the 4-Winged Framework© addresses. This framework now offers executive coaches and other stakeholders of the coaching industry a structured yet flexible lens through which to locate themselves, make meaning of the changes they face, and begin to chart a grounded way forward in the digital age.

The 4-Winged Framework© fills a critical gap in the coaching literature to understand digitalisation, not just as a technological shift, but as a socio-contextual force deeply reshaping the terrain of executive coaching. The findings suggest that executive coaches are not unaware of this transformation. On the contrary, many demonstrate a high degree of awareness and appreciation for the profound impact digitalisation is likely to have on their profession. Yet, despite this awareness, most coaches acknowledged a limited understanding of the phenomenon itself. This gap is understandable: few have received formal training on digitalisation, and there is a striking lack of literature that offers any cohesive articulation of its implications for coaching. As a result, even seasoned professionals found themselves without the vocabulary or conceptual tools to engage meaningfully with these changes. There was, however, an unmistakable appetite for clarity. Respondents expressed a keen interest in the findings of this research as a way to make sense of their lived realities and navigate what lies ahead.

This absence of shared language has implications beyond the coaching community. It creates a situation in which coaches, and equally, clients, coach training institutes, accreditation bodies, HR leaders, L&D professionals, and even buyers of coaching services, struggle to describe, explore, or even recognise what is unfolding. One of the highly experienced executive coaches captured this ambiguity with disarming honesty when asked how digitalisation might impact his work: "F%$k knows". His response may have lacked technical terminology, but it powerfully expressed the broader sense of confusion and uncertainty. Similarly, the opening story of my telecom CXO client, who struggled to name the very disruption she was experiencing, suggests that this lack of vocabulary extends across all participants in the coaching conversation.

In this context, the 4-Winged Framework© is more than just a model, it becomes a shared map. One that helps executive coaches locate their experiences, name the shifts they are witnessing, and engage in more grounded, generative dialogue about how their profession is evolving.

7.2 Using the 4-Winged Framework©

In his foundational work on symbolic interactionism, Blumer (1969) argued that human action is shaped by the meanings people assign to the phenomena they encounter. In that spirit, the four conceptual categories that emerged from this research, grounded in the lived experiences of executive coaches, now offer more than just insight. Along with the thick descriptions summarised in Table 7.1, they provide a much-needed vocabulary for the coaching ecosystem. Practitioners, researchers, supervisors, educators, and buyers of coaching can now begin to make meaning of digitalisation not in abstract terms, but in a language that resonates with the realities of their work.

The maxim from the philosophy of language, that "we do not describe the world we see; we see the world we know how to describe", is particularly relevant here. So too is the Sapir-Whorf hypothesis of linguistic relativity (Kay & Kempton, 1984), which suggests that the language we possess can shape our perception of the world around us. Without a shared lexicon or structured way to frame the impact of digitalisation, much of the coaching profession has remained in a reactive stance, aware of change but unsure how to grasp or articulate it.

This is where the 4-Winged Framework© hopes to contribute meaningfully. By offering a vocabulary and an organising structure, it can support more informed, intentional conversations across the coaching landscape. I hope that this framework will serve as both a mirror and a map: a mirror that reflects the nuanced and often complex experiences of executive coaches in the digital age, and a map that helps various stakeholders, coaches, clients, HR leaders, supervisors, educators, training institutes, and accreditation bodies, navigate these changes with greater clarity and confidence.

A shared conceptual framework creates more than just structure; it fosters a sense of comprehension and security that is essential for navigating a phenomenon as diffuse and disruptive as digitalisation. One of the coaches I interviewed put it simply: "Digital is something which, in my view, is so poorly defined, there is no standard understanding". That lack of clarity has hampered meaningful engagement across both coaching practice and research. In that light, the frameworks presented across this book, particularly in Figures 3.1, 7.1, and 7.2, aim to reduce that sense of ambiguity. They offer a foundation upon which the coaching profession can build a deeper understanding and more proactive response to the socio-contextual forces reshaping its future.

It is helpful to view all the frameworks presented in this book as maps, guiding structures rather than fixed prescriptions. As Brown (2021) aptly reminds us, "With an adventurous heart and the right maps, we can travel anywhere and never fear losing ourselves". In a landscape as dynamic and uncharted as the one shaped by digitalisation, such maps are not luxuries, they are necessities. The 4-Winged Framework©, along with the conceptual foundations laid in earlier chapters, offers exactly this kind of map. These maps do not claim to be definitive, but provide language, structure, and starting points. Given the wide-ranging and layered impact of digitalisation, as encountered, experienced, felt, and responded to by executive coaches, it becomes essential that this conversation extends beyond individual practitioners.

Coach training institutes, supervisors, accreditation institutes, professional bodies, and organisational sponsors all have a stake in this evolving narrative. If the coaching profession is to remain relevant, credible, and human-centred in the face of rapid digital change, it must develop a shared vocabulary and conceptual toolkit to make sense of what is unfolding.

We now turn to the next chapter, where we explore how executive coaches can begin to *navigate the future*, not just by responding to change, but actively shaping what comes next. But before that, it is worth spending time with the exercises to start using the framework for yourself.

Reflective Exercise 7.1 Using the 4-Winged Framework©

Now that you are familiar with the 4-Winged Framework©, take time to reflect on your own coaching journey through its lens. This model isn't just a conceptual map, it's a mirror. It helps you see where you stand, how you've responded to digitalisation so far, and where new awareness or growth may be needed.

Whether you're a coach, a supervisor, a coach educator, a buyer of coaching services, or part of a training body, this reflection can anchor your next steps with greater clarity and confidence. Go over the four steps below to start using the framework.

Step 1: Locate Yourself: Which of the four areas resonates most with your current coaching experience?

- *Encountering Change*—Are you feeling the friction of new technologies entering your coaching space? Is your agenda with clients changing?
- *Experiencing Loss of Depth*—Do you feel that your connection with clients has shifted online—perhaps feeling less embodied, spontaneous, or safe?
- *Imagining Irrelevance*—Are you concerned about being replaced by AI? Are questions of relevance, value, or future-readiness showing up in your practice?
- *Navigating the Future*—Are you experimenting with new formats, tools, or ideas? Are you actively exploring what a flourishing coaching practice might look like in the digital age?

Circle or name one (or more) wings that feel most alive for you right now.

Step 2: Revisit a Moment: Can you recall a specific coaching interaction that exemplifies your experience in this area (as selected in the previous exercise)? Describe it briefly:

- What happened?
- What digital element (or absence of one) was involved?
- What assumptions, fears, or hopes did this situation evoke in you?
- How did you respond?

This isn't about judging your reaction, but noticing the patterns of response you bring to this shifting landscape.

Step 3: Consider What You Need: What other resources or support might help you navigate this wing more confidently? You might consider:

- Supervision or peer consultation to metabolise complexity or discomfort.
- CPD opportunities focused on coaching presence in virtual spaces or emerging tech.
- Platform training to reduce anxiety and increase fluency.
- Research or writing groups to help you articulate and engage with these themes.

If you're a coach, educator, or supervisor, consider how you might integrate these themes into your curriculum or mentoring. If you're part of a corporate L&D function, think about how these dimensions might shape your expectations of coaching partnerships.

Step 4: Imagine an Intentional Response: Where might you lean in more intentionally next?

- Is it time to update your practice to meet emerging needs?
- Do you need to pause and re-ground yourself before venturing further?
- Could you initiate a community conversation with fellow coaches to collectively process change?

Let the framework act as both a mirror and a compass. It helps you notice where you are—and opens possibilities for where you might wish to go.

Reflective Exercise 7.2 Developing Your Own Frameworks

The 4-Winged Framework© is one lens to explore the digital impact on coaching. But each coach, educator, or coaching stakeholder has their own context. What might your framework look like?

Sketch out your own three to four element framework for understanding or navigating digitalisation in coaching. You may want to consider:

- What are the most pressing digital realities in your context?
- How do these affect coaching conversations, goals, or relationships?
- What capacities, tools, or values do you believe must be preserved or developed?
- What role could your framework play, in your team, in training spaces, or with clients?

This is not about "getting it right", but about deepening your ability to see, name, and work with what matters most in your own ecosystem. Your framework might just be the spark that others need to begin their own.

References

Aguinaldo, J. P. (2004). Rethinking validity in qualitative research from a social constructionist perspective: From "Is this valid research?" to "What is this research valid for?" *The Qualitative Report*, *9*(1), 127.

Alavi, S., Abd. Wahab, D., Muhamad, N., & Arbab Shirani, B. (2014). Organic structure and organisational learning as the main antecedents of workforce agility. *International Journal of Production Research*, *52*(21), 6273–6295.

Avolio, B. J., Sosik, J. J., Kahai, S. S., & Baker, B. (2014). E-leadership: Re-examining transformations in leadership source and transmission. *The Leadership Quarterly*, *25*(1), 105–131.

Blumer, H. (1969). *Symbolic interactionism: Perspective and method*. California University Press.

Brown, B. (2021). *Atlas of the heart: Mapping meaningful connection and the language of human experience*. Random House.

Bryant, A. (2002). Re-grounding grounded theory. *Journal of Information Technology Theory and Application (JITTA)*, *4*(1), 7.

Charmaz, K. (2014). *Constructing grounded theory*. Sage.

Colbert, A., Yee, N., & George, G. (2016). The digital workforce and the workplace of the future. *Academy of Management Perspectives*, *30*(2), 156–165.

Cortellazzo, L., Bruni, E., & Zampieri, R. (2019). The role of leadership in a digitalized world: A review. *Frontiers in Psychology*, *10*, 1938.

Henriette, E., Feki, M., & Boughzala, I. (2016). Digital transformation challenges. In *Proceedings of the 10th Mediterranean Conference on Information Systems (MCIS 2016)*. Paphos, Cyprus, September 3–5.

Kane, G. C., Phillips, A. N., Copulsky, J., & Andrus, G. (2019). How digital leadership is(n't) different. *MIT Sloan Management Review*, *60*(3), 34–39.

Kay, P., & Kempton, W. (1984). What is the Sapir-Whorf hypothesis? *American Anthropologist*, *86*(1), 65–79.

Khan, S. (2016). *Leadership in the digital age: A study on the effects of digitalisation on top management leadership* (Master's thesis, Stockholm University).

Mohammad, K. (2009). E-leadership: The emerging new leadership for the virtual organization. *Journal of Managerial Sciences*, *3*(1), 1–16.

Parviainen, P., Tihinen, M., Kääriäinen, J., & Teppola, S. (2017). Tackling the digitalization challenge: How to benefit from digitalization in practice. *International Journal of Information Systems and Project Management*, *5*(1), 63–77.

Qiu, Y., & Pesch, R. (2019). The impact of digitalisation on organisations: A review of the empirical literature. *Academy of Management Proceedings*, *2019*(1), 16207.

Schwab, K. (2016). *The fourth industrial revolution*. World Economic Forum.

Vey, K., Fandel-Meyer, T., Zipp, J. S., & Schneider, C. (2017). Learning & development in times of digital transformation: Facilitating a culture of change and innovation. *International Journal of Advanced Corporate Learning*, *10*(1), 22–32.

8 Navigating the Future

8.1 Creating a Coaching Continuum©

The findings of my study underscore that changes and advancements in the digital landscape can evoke both fear and anxiety among executive coaches. Yet, nestled alongside these concerns is a strong sense of optimism and hope, a belief in the enduring value of coaching, and in its potential to evolve meaningfully in response to digital change. This coexistence of apprehension and assurance, of dread and confidence, presents not a contradiction but, as one respondent aptly described it, "an unmixed blessing".

Scholars (Dent & Goldberg, 1999; Piderit, 2000) have argued that formal studies on *resistance to change* have often missed the nuances of such complex responses. Merron (1993), in fact, called for retiring the term "resistance to change" altogether, on both philosophical and practical grounds (Dent & Goldberg, 1999). Piderit (2000) suggested a more ***multidimensional view of how individuals respond to change***, distinguishing between emotional, cognitive, and intentional reactions. From this perspective, support for change reflects ***positive responses across all three dimensions***, while resistance reflects the opposite.

In earlier chapters, particularly Chapters 4 and 6, we explored the emotional undercurrents of unease, disconnection, and even irrelevance felt by many coaches. This chapter shifts the lens. Here, we turn to those moments of **optimism, creativity, and constructive engagement** that emerged from the findings. It is these affirmative responses that form the foundation for what comes next, a framework for understanding how digital tools support coaching in the digital age.

What distinguishes the insights shared in this chapter is that they go beyond the reactive posture many coaches were forced into during the pandemic. Instead, this chapter highlights a proactive and imaginative orientation, where coaches are beginning to integrate digital tools

DOI: 10.4324/9781003638834-12

intentionally into their ways of working, sometimes in subtle ways, sometimes in transformative ones.

This constructive shift first became evident when coaches spoke about staying connected with clients between sessions. While some preferred to maintain firm boundaries and limited this communication to email, others described using messaging apps for light-touch follow-ups, reminders, or sharing updates. As Rohan explained: "I coach you, let's say for one hour, one and a half hours, once in a month… between the time I talked to you now to the time I talk to you later. I'm now in touch with you, maybe an email. Maybe you might send me a chat".

Many coaches described these asynchronous exchanges, where neither party needs to schedule a meeting, as uniquely beneficial. Even coaches who largely work in synchronous modes (face-to-face or live virtual sessions) found value in the flexibility, brevity, and frequency of such digital touchpoints. A few even referred to these exchanges as "micro coaching sessions". One coach suggested they might "change the model of coaching a little bit, so that there'll be shorter, sharper interactions".

Crucially, these were not seen as replacements for in-depth coaching conversations but as complementary moments that extended the coaching relationship beyond traditional, bounded sessions. These micro-interactions, brief messages, check-ins, nudges, and reflections, formed what I began to visualise as a coaching continuum: an extended, dynamic engagement between coach and client that moves fluidly across formats, durations, and depths. It was this recurring idea of continuity, a thread of coaching presence carried between formats, durations, and depths, that inspired the conceptualisation of a model for what such a continuum could look like in practice. This is shared as Table 8.2. But rather than rushing to this continuum model, let me build towards it gradually, by unpacking the logic that underpins it and sharing examples of how coaches are already beginning to work in this more fluid, digitally augmented way.

A few respondents highlighted that the topics some clients brought into coaching sessions did not always require a full sixty- or ninety-minute conversation. In such instances, they saw clear value in quick, focused interactions that could address the client's immediate need without the formality of a full session. Gloria described this as "SOS coaching"—"I think it has been a bit like SOS coaching. That's just been often reminding people how resilient they are". In another moment of reflection, she added: "This feels relatively straightforward... the stuff that actually, I think, you know what, there's not some deep issue here that we've got to go into and untangle".

This notion of short, sharp engagements, offered in moments of urgency resonated with other coaches as well. These quick interactions, often enabled by digital messaging or short video calls, were seen not as replacements for the longer, deeper sessions but as complementary touchpoints. Coaches consistently emphasised that such brief encounters worked best when placed alongside traditional sessions, forming part of a broader, more responsive coaching relationship. Conversations in these short sessions also included discussions on pricing. While several coaches acknowledged that these shorter sessions might eventually call for a different pricing model, none had formally adopted such changes yet. For now, these mini-sessions were largely offered within the boundaries of the existing coaching relationship, more as value-adding extensions than standalone offerings.

While most of my respondents had by now incorporated video-mediated coaching in their repertoire (Garratt et al., 2022), digital tools that support asynchronous communication have yet to see similar levels of adoption. There is a growing body of scholarly debate on the efficacy of remote coaching (Berry, 2005; Berry et al., 2011; Charbonneau, 2002), but significantly less attention has been given to the role of asynchronous communication in executive coaching. The limited research in this space (Boyce & Clutterbuck, 2010; Passarelli et al., 2020) tends to draw from broader theoretical lenses such as Media Richness Theory (MRT) and Human-Automation Interaction (HAI).

MRT suggests that richer media, those allowing for immediate feedback, multiple cues, and personal focus, are more effective for complex and equivocal communication. From that lens, asynchronous communication might seem to fall short. However, *HAI perspectives* offer a more nuanced view. Research in this field supports the use of asynchronous digital tools in learning and development settings, particularly where the learner exhibits strong intrinsic motivation (Bailey et al., 2021). These theories propose that asynchronous interactions, when situated within meaningful relational contexts, can become powerful complements rather than substitutes for real-time engagement.

The findings of my study reinforce this view. Executive coaches are beginning to experiment with asynchronous communication as a way to extend the coaching container, to maintain touchpoints, reinforce accountability, and allow for brief yet meaningful exchanges between longer sessions. Asynchronous updates, nudges, and reflections offer continuity and momentum while respecting both coach and client time.

HAI research also explores how non-synchronous and non-verbal interactions can still offer a sense of relational presence and engagement (Pfeifer & Scheier, 2001). In the context of coaching in the digital age, this offers exciting possibilities. As we build towards a **Coaching Continuum©**, these tools could help coaches move from a strictly session-based practice to a more fluid and responsive model, where synchronous and asynchronous elements work in tandem, supporting a more holistic coaching relationship.

Another area where respondents saw potential for digital tools and apps was in fostering creativity, play, and experimentation during coaching sessions. Many suggested that the traditional, face-to-face setup, often limited to just a pen and paper, constrained the possibilities for dynamic engagement. In contrast, the digital coaching environment, with an active computer as part of the setup, seemed to unlock a range of opportunities. As Gloria observed, "Working in a digital world enables, encourages, and forces far more experimentation".

Several coaches highlighted how the functionalities of video conferencing platforms, combined with ready access to resources, allowed them to share materials with clients in real time,whether it was a relevant YouTube clip, a quote from a book, or an article that deepened the client's reflection. These digital exchanges were not mere conveniences; they became springboards for richer, more layered conversations. Importantly, coaches also acknowledged that this mode of coaching was different. It required new skills and ways of thinking. A few described how they were beginning to experiment with collaborative tools that allowed drawing, sketching, or co-creating visuals during the session. As one coach shared, "I've had some experience with technology to provide collaboration and create a creative environment. So, using features on the iPad where you can draw and... that kind of thing, we're learning about it. We're learning new skills, new methods... I think there's lots of really exciting technology that can be quite fun to use and is intuitive".

Such examples suggest that digital tools are not just add-ons, they are enablers of a different kind of coaching experience. One that extends beyond conversation into shared exploration. The coach and client are no longer just exchanging words; they are co-constructing meaning, often through other forms of interaction—visual, tactile, and creative.

Sanjay took this idea even further. Reflecting on the potential of digital tools, he suggested that in the emerging digital age, "the executive coach's role is no longer conversational, it now needs to become quasi-experimental". An interesting provocation. And one that invites us to reimagine what's possible when coaching embraces a spirit of experimentation, fuelled by the digital tools at our fingertips.

Inspired by these examples, Table 8.1 offers a list of commonly available digital tools that coaches are already beginning to use. These are not the most sophisticated technologies, those are evolving rapidly and arriving almost every day, but even this basic set gives us a glimpse into the exciting territory we're stepping into. Their applications hint at how digital tools can quietly but meaningfully extend the coaching space and shape its future possibilities.

This table is not meant to be exhaustive. Rather, it points to the simple, everyday technologies that are already within reach, and already reshaping how coaching is done. As newer tools emerge, the invitation for coaches is not just to adopt them passively but to experiment thoughtfully and integrate them meaningfully into their practice.

Table 8.1 Common Digital Tools and Suggested Applications

Tools	*Application*
Screen Sharing	Coaches can use these functions to share their screens with clients during live video sessions. This enables them to illustrate concepts, walk through visuals, offer feedback, or discuss ideas using existing content or tools.
Whiteboarding	Digital whiteboards allow coaches and clients to co-create in real time, whether for brainstorming, planning, mapping, or reflective exercises. The collaborative nature of whiteboarding can invite deeper client engagement and playful exploration.
Note-taking	While many coaches still prefer pen and paper, digital note-taking tools offer a convenient way to track session highlights, client progress, or emerging patterns. However, caution is advised, coaches must stay present, as overreliance on typing or recording can detract from relational presence.
Time-keeping	Time-tracking tools help coaches manage session durations precisely, ensuring both structure and billing transparency. They are especially useful in shorter or back-to-back virtual sessions.

Building on similar principles, the past decade has witnessed the rise of several dedicated online coaching platforms (Kanatouri, 2020). These differ from general-purpose collaboration or creativity tools in both intent and function. In the context of coaching, the term *platform* carries a different connotation than its typical use in information technology. Rather than referring to infrastructure-level ecosystems (Gawer & Cusumano, 2014), in coaching research and practice, platforms typically refer to digital tools or software environments designed with an exclusive focus on helping coaches structure, organise, and manage their coaching relationships and businesses more effectively. These platforms often offer features such as session scheduling, note-taking, client dashboards, progress tracking, and integrated communication tools, all within one unified interface. Yet, despite their growing presence in the market, awareness and adoption among executive coaches in this study appeared limited. While a few respondents acknowledged the existence of such platforms, none had used them in their own practice. This absence may be explained, at least in part, by the demographic profile of the interviewees, most were seasoned practitioners who had established their coaching practices well before such platforms were developed, and had little perceived need to shift away from their existing systems.

What was perhaps more surprising, however, was that even the more technologically inclined coaches had not explored these platforms. Whether due to habit, scepticism, lack of training, or a limited perception of added value, these tools remained largely peripheral to the respondents' current practice. This points to a potentially fertile area for further exploration and targeted coach development. How might these platforms evolve to genuinely support the relational, reflective, and dynamic nature of executive coaching? And what might it take for experienced coaches to view them not merely as administrative add-ons, but as integral extensions of their professional practice?

Would this shift require a different kind of CPD offering, or even a new pricing model that aligns platform-based coaching with evolving client expectations? While the findings highlight a current gap in both support and structured development opportunities related to digital tools, they also reveal a positive underlying orientation. At a broader level, the executive coaches in this study expressed openness towards technological advances and a willingness to explore. As one coach put it, they were "open to that and willing to experiment". Taken together, the findings point to a growing interest among executive coaches in both synchronous and asynchronous digital tools, marking the beginning of a shift, rather than its culmination.

While discussing digital tools, an adjacent conversation emerged around pricing strategies. Several executive coaches observed that smaller, on-demand sessions (SOS coaching) might warrant a different rate structure, though none had implemented this yet. More commonly, coaches contrasted virtual with in-person fees. Given the additional time, travel, and logistical effort required for face-to-face meetings, many felt justified in charging premium rates. As one coach explained, "If I travel to your office, it takes me an hour each way. For a one-hour session, I'd end up billing three hours of time, that isn't feasible. By moving sessions online, a one-hour appointment stays a one-hour appointment, which makes pricing straightforward".

Some coaches further proposed a tiered pricing model that aligns digital tools within a broader portfolio. Under this continuum, face-to-face sessions carry the highest fee, virtual sessions a standard rate, and app-based support is offered at lower price points. Each element plays a distinct role in the overall coaching journey, yet all integrate seamlessly around the core one-to-one session. As Kylie illustrated using the example of a popular meditation app, "and I think there is a case for that. It's an app, and it doesn't provide the depth of interaction, but it brings a human voice, a very human approach, so it works. We can't possibly call it coaching, but it forms part of the toolset I offer. I refer clients to it; it becomes part of the whole package, possibly engaging different generations or client segments".

This approach of framing digital tools as communication channels or differing modes to connect with executive coaching clients suggests that visualising traditional coaching alongside these emerging digital options as part of a larger coaching continuum could help understand how the future of coaching in the digital age might evolve. In Table 8.2, I provide one such framework of Coaching Continuum©.

This framework is constructed by positioning various channels like face-to-face, video, telephone, text, and apps and bots on the x-axis. The variables that could govern the mode choice are plotted on the y-axis. This framework proposes one possible visualisation of a coaching continuum, which executive coaches see as the future of coaching in the digital age.

Table 8.2 Coaching Continuum©

	Constructing a Coaching Continuum©				
Mode of Coaching >> Variables to Consider	***Face to Face***	***Through VC***	***Telephone***	***Text Based***	***Apps & Bots***
Price Fee for the client	££££	£££	££	£	£ (?) Possible to have free options
Organisational **Hierarchy**	CEO, Board	CXO	Senior Management	Middle Management	Everyone in the Organisation
Temporality of Coaching Sessions	First Session Longer Sessions	Post First Session Shorter Session	After F2F or VC Sessions Shorter	Between Sessions Really Short	Anytime, Even After the End of EC Engagement Customized
Formalization	Structured		Informal	On Demand Dip In and Out	
Depth Senses Used	All Senses	Hearing and Seeing	Hearing	Reading and Typing	Hearing—Speaking or Reading—Typing
Age Attitude to Tech	Older Digital Immigrants				Younger Digital Natives
Kind of Coaching	Ontological		Results and Skills		Behavioural Goal Attainment

The Coaching Continuum© table proposes that the choice of medium be informed by a set of coaching-related variables.

It may be useful to think of the vertical lines not as fixed barriers, but as permeable boundaries that shift with context. This acknowledges the fluid nature of many categories, which are often not rigidly tied to any one coaching mode. For instance, CEOs and CXOs may prefer face-to-face interactions, yet they could also engage meaningfully via text, apps, or bots. Conversely, younger clients, often assumed to be digital natives, might still value the depth and nuance of in-person dialogue. While tentative and evolving, the Coaching Continuum© provides a practical, practitioner-informed framework for coaching in the digital age.

One coach's suggestion to "price" virtual sessions differently, "make it as affordable as possible"—illustrates the kind of flexible thinking embedded in this continuum. This framework also accounts for a sliding price scale, adaptable to different coaching modalities. Another described the value of "shorter, sharper interactions", which highlights the "temporality" variable. The idea of "SOS Coaching" brings immediacy and responsiveness into view. The continuum further incorporates the advantages of asynchronous communication, its succinctness and flexibility, into the broader coaching experience.

The variable of "depth" acknowledges the limitations of virtual modes, particularly in capturing subtle cues. One coach's remark about the "inability to smell" encapsulates this perceived loss of sensory richness. Yet, instead of dismissing digital modes, the continuum now invites coaches to consider how each mode can serve a particular purpose, within a thoughtful and intentional coaching architecture.

Seen through the lens of access, affordability, and adaptability, the *Coaching Continuum©* begins to offer more than just convenience, it hints at a shift in how coaching can be delivered, experienced, and scaled. With lower entry costs, reduced logistical barriers, and the possibility of on-demand support, digital modes of coaching open new doors for clients who may have previously found coaching inaccessible. This reconfiguration of coaching's architecture doesn't dilute its essence; instead, it expands its reach. And it is this very potential—to extend the impact of coaching beyond traditional confines, that we now explore in the next section: the democratisation of coaching.

8.2 Democratisation of Coaching

It often strikes me as strange, and at times, frustrating, that a profession grounded in helping others grow and thrive, remains, in many ways, deeply elitist. For all its growth and visibility, executive coaching largely continues to serve a narrow demographic: senior leaders in large, often global, corporations. Despite its effectiveness, coaching has not yet evolved into a widespread tool for social transformation. I see little organised movement to use coaching as an agent of social change, as Shoukry and Cox (2018) have argued it could be. Nor do I see pathways that would allow a small business owner in rural India or a micro-entrepreneur in Ghana to access coaching in any sustained or meaningful way. While many coaches do offer pro-bono engagements, the scale and scope of these efforts remain limited and, in some cases, symbolic.

Interestingly, the findings from this study reveal that many coaches themselves recognise this imbalance. They acknowledge that the current structure of executive coaching, its pricing models, positioning, and delivery mechanisms, can contribute to a perception of elitism and exclusivity. They also express cautious optimism that digital access and new technological tools may create opportunities to broaden coaching's reach. Before exploring what this potential future might look like, it is important to unpack the charge of elitism often directed at executive coaching, and hear what coaches themselves have to say about it.

Some respondents argued that the perceived exclusivity of executive coaching might actually contribute to its appeal among CXOs and senior leaders. According to them, the very structure of executive coaching, personalised, high-touch, and often high-cost, can reinforce a sense of importance and feed into the egos of those at the top. The causality, however, was less clear. Was it the exclusivity of the process that made it attractive to senior leaders? Or was it the fact that only senior leaders could afford and access such services that gave it an aura of exclusivity in the first place?

Regardless of where one places the causal arrow, what emerged from the research was this: executive coaching, as it currently exists in most organisations, is a resource reserved almost exclusively for the top echelons. As one coach reflected, "if it's because of the exclusivity that might be attached to the executive coaching relationship, that might have driven that [appeal for CXOs]". Another coach added, "Some people in those very senior, elite environments like to have somebody who's well-regarded", and, by implication, expensive.

This dynamic, where the higher the rank, the higher the fee, only deepens the perception of coaching as an elitist practice. One respondent went so far as to suggest that the very idea of scaling coaching widely was at odds with the premium nature of the service. In his view, high-quality coaching work, delivered by highly experienced coaches, would always command a high price. Given the limited number of such coaches and continued demand from senior executives, he argued that price would remain a structural barrier to democratising coaching.

Beyond cost, another reason offered for restricting coaching to senior leaders was their perceived level of autonomy. Some argue that coaching only makes sense when the client has the authority and freedom to act on the insights that emerge. As one coach put it: "Coaching made a lot more sense where the person concerned actually had a level of autonomy in how they functioned... If the person is not in a position to do something about it, it becomes extremely frustrating, for them and for me". While this may sound reasonable, it also carries an implicit bias, that only those in leadership roles have the capacity to translate reflection into action. That assumption, however, is not supported by research and deserves to be questioned more deeply.

It was fascinating to hear arguments around price and quality being presented by executive coaches themselves as barriers to democratising coaching, especially considering that every single respondent also acknowledged how profoundly helpful coaching was and how important it is to scale it more broadly. Hearing these two ideas, "coaching must be scaled" and "coaching cannot be scaled because of quality and price", offered in the same breath made me pause. It led me to wonder: are these real, structural barriers, or are they subtle ways of defending the status quo? Are these hesitations genuine concerns, or are they symptoms of an industry grappling with the fear of being disrupted?

History shows us that such arguments are not unique to coaching. In fact, they are almost always raised by incumbents in any industry facing the early signs of innovation or disruption. The argument goes something like this: *the service we offer is premium, requires skill, cannot be mass-produced without loss of quality, and is therefore rightfully expensive*. This has echoed across sectors, from education and health care to finance and telecom. And yet, time and again, new entrants have come in and rewritten the rules.

I have seen this up close. In my own professional experience, two powerful examples come to mind—*M-Pesa* in Africa and *Jio* in India. M-Pesa radically transformed financial inclusion in East Africa by allowing users to send and receive money through basic mobile phones, no internet, no smartphone, no bank account. At its inception, M-Pesa faced intense resistance from traditional banks, who argued that such a service was too risky, too low-quality, and couldn't be trusted with people's money. But within a few years, it had enabled millions of unbanked individuals to participate in the formal economy, faster, safer, and cheaper than before. Jio's entry into India's telecom sector followed a similar arc. Established telecom players insisted that quality service required significant investment and therefore had to come at a premium. Jio dismantled this assumption by offering voice calls for free and data at prices never seen before, forcing the entire industry to rethink its pricing and service models. Today, India is one of the lowest-cost data markets in the world, and digital access has spread dramatically across social and economic divides.

Similar stories abound across industries. Khan Academy and Duolingo have disrupted elite tutoring. Telemedicine platforms like Practo and 1mg in India have challenged the assumption that quality healthcare requires physical proximity. In each case, incumbents raised concerns about quality, safety, and cost. And in each case, it was not these barriers but their own mindset that turned out to be the biggest obstacle.

This pattern aligns closely with what Christensen (1997) famously called *The Innovator's Dilemma*. He argued that established players often struggle to adopt disruptive technologies, not because they don't see the change coming, but because they are trapped by their own success. Their business models, pricing structures, and definitions of value are so deeply embedded that anything which threatens to alter them is instinctively viewed as a threat rather than an opportunity. As a result, incumbents find excuses; disruptors find openings. Hence, the arguments put forth by experienced coaches about why coaching cannot be scaled start to look less like objective constraints and more like a classic case of the innovator's dilemma. Christensen (1997) observed that established players often reject or delay engagement with disruptive innovations not because they lack vision, but because they are bound by the very systems that made them successful, pricing models, client expectations, and narrow definitions of quality and value. These systems become constraints rather than enablers.

Earlier in this chapter, Table 8.2 presented a more expansive view of what coaching in the digital age might look like. The *Coaching Continuum©*, it proposed, is not merely a chart of options, it is a mindset shift. It asks us to stop seeing coaching as a one-size-fits-all, 90-minute session with a senior leader, and instead begin viewing it as a spectrum of engagements: from high-touch, face-to-face interactions to short, sharp, asynchronous nudges via messaging apps or curated digital content. It shows how pricing can vary across this spectrum, with each mode offering a different value proposition and level of accessibility. Importantly, it reveals how coaching can be made more affordable, more frequent, and more embedded in day-to-day leadership practice, without necessarily diluting its core purpose.

The question, then, is not whether coaching can be democratised. The tools, models, and technological infrastructure to do so already exist. The real question is whether the coaching profession, its practitioners, buyers, and training institutions, will choose to adopt more inclusive frameworks like the *Coaching Continuum©*, or resist them under the banner of tradition and quality. Will the industry protect its current definitions of value, or reimagine its role in a more accessible and digitally mediated future? The answer to that may well determine whether coaching becomes a force for broader leadership development, or remains a preserve of the privileged few.

A few respondents were especially blunt about the vested interests within the current ecosystem of executive coaching that may be preventing meaningful disruption. One posed a piercing question: "Who gets threatened most by democracy? It's the people in power". Another reflected on why established coaches might be less enthusiastic about democratising the practice: "You think about it as a socio-technical process... or it's about power and the implementation of power". Beneath these remarks lies a tension, the promise of coaching as a tool for transformation and its current embodiment as a premium service reserved for a privileged few.

While these debates exposed underlying power dynamics, the overwhelming majority of respondents expressed a belief that executive coaching should be made more accessible. Yet, they often seemed to be waiting for someone else to lead the change. They saw the potential of coaching to enable deeper reflection, transformation, and even social change, well beyond the narrow confines of boardrooms and C-suites, but hesitated to see themselves as the ones to drive that expansion. Most admitted they neither had the time, energy, nor inclination to disrupt the current model from within.

As a result, it is increasingly likely that the real disruption to the coaching industry will arrive from the outside. And the first barrier to fall will almost certainly be cost, as it did in the cases of M-Pesa, Jio, Khan Academy or 1mg. The findings of this study suggest that digital tools and platforms offer a credible and scalable way to bring down the price of coaching. In doing so, they also chip away at its perceived elitism. Coaching, when made affordable, need not remain the preserve of senior executives. It can become a broader developmental resource across organisations.

Moreover, a more democratised coaching ecosystem opens up powerful possibilities for social change. When coaching becomes accessible to a wider cross-section of leaders, especially those embedded in local, social, and cultural complexities, the practice becomes more relevant and more humane. It allows the coaching conversation to stretch beyond work-based goals into the lived realities of the client's social world. This is where digitalisation becomes even more meaningful, not just in reducing cost, but in overcoming the second major barrier: physical location and access. The following case from Gloria illustrates this well.

Connecting from Home—A Different Kind of Conversation (Case Study 8)

Gloria shared an experience that illustrates how the physical setting of a coaching conversation can influence its emotional depth. She was working with a senior executive, a CXO, who, despite being committed to the coaching process, rarely opened up during their office-based sessions. The environment was private and confidential, yet something about it seemed to restrain the client's openness.

Things changed dramatically when a coaching session was conducted virtually while the client was working from home. Gloria recalled: "That coaching session was then in her own home, and I wonder if there was something about the safety and the security and the comfort in a familiar environment that enabled her to be more open and more vulnerable in that coaching session".

In this new setting, a wider range of personal topics surfaced, issues that had never emerged in the corporate office. Gloria and her client explored areas that were deeply important to her as a person, not just as a professional. The session took an unexpected turn when the conversation led to her daughter, who was struggling with learning difficulties at college. Gloria helped the client connect with a specialised coach who could support her daughter, something the client hadn't previously considered bringing into the coaching space. "I don't think such an engagement would have been possible from her office", was Gloria's take.

This case illustrates how digital tools can lower physical and psychological barriers, enabling deeper, more personal coaching conversations. Shifting the session from a formal office to the client's home created a safe, familiar space that allowed greater openness and led to unexpected but meaningful outcomes. It reinforces the need to democratise coaching by making it more accessible and context-sensitive, beyond corporate settings and senior roles, through the thoughtful use of digital platforms.

If coaching is to become more than a developmental tool for the privileged few, its future must be both inclusive and intentional. I suggest that democratising coaching is no longer a utopian idea; it is a practical possibility, made viable by digital tools, lower cost structures, and scalable delivery models. When coaching reaches leaders and changemakers beyond the boardroom, those in schools, in start-ups, in community enterprises, it begins to unlock its deeper potential: not just to support individual success but to catalyse social transformation. This is where the true power of coaching lies: in helping people navigate complexity, connect meaningfully, and act with greater awareness in their contexts.

If we reimagine Coaching as a Continuum©, flexible in format, accessible in price, and responsive to context, it can evolve from a bespoke service into a movement. One that enables not only better leaders, but better systems and societies. That, perhaps, is the most hopeful promise of digitalisation in coaching, not just to scale access, but to scale impact.

Reflective Exercise 8.1 Designing Your Own Coaching Continuum©

This reflection invites you to stretch your imagination, and your practice, across the full spectrum of coaching possibilities in the digital age.

1. **Take Stock: How Are You Showing Up Today?** List the modes you currently use in your coaching practice (e.g., face-to-face, video, phone, messaging, email, apps). Now ask yourself:
   - Which mode do I lean on most, and why?
   - Which one feels underused or underexplored?
   - Where might I be playing too safe?
2. **Explore the Coaching Variables** (as per the Coaching Continuum Framework©). Using the model as inspiration, reflect on these dimensions:
   - **Depth**: Which modes allow you to explore deeper issues? Where do you feel a loss of depth?
   - **Temporality**: Are you offering any shorter, "SOS-style" interactions? Could these complement your traditional sessions?
   - **Access**: Who might you be unintentionally excluding due to your current mode preferences?

- **Pricing**: How are your modes currently priced (or bundled)? Are there creative pricing options you've considered but not yet trialled?

3. **Sketch Your Evolving Map**. Grab a pen (or your favourite digital tool) and draw your own personal Coaching Continuum©.
   - Place your modes across a horizontal axis. Add the variables (depth, access, etc.) vertically.
   - Now map: Where are you now, and where do you want to grow?
4. **Try One Bold Shift**. Choose one practical shift you can try in the next 30–60 days.
   - Add a short asynchronous touchpoint between sessions?
   - Pilot a hybrid pricing model?
   - Test an app-supported coaching package with a willing client?

Even a small experiment can begin to reshape your coaching for the digital age.

Reflective Exercise 8.2 Reimagining Coaching for a Wider World

Executive coaching has often been confined to the boardrooms and the privileged few. But as this chapter explored, digital tools, changing attitudes, and new delivery models now offer a real opportunity to expand coaching's reach and impact. This exercise invites you to reflect on your role and your responsibility in shaping that future.

1. **Scan Your Practice**: Who currently benefits from your coaching? What kind of clients do you typically serve, and what does that say about the accessibility of your work?
2. **Challenge Your Assumptions**: Reflect on any internal beliefs you might hold about who is "ready" or "suitable" for coaching. Are these beliefs grounded in evidence, or shaped by industry norms and commercial pressures?
3. **Reimagine Access**: Think about one group, community, or context, perhaps geographically distant, resource-constrained, or traditionally excluded, where coaching could make a difference. How might digital tools help you reach them?

4. **Design for Inclusion**: If you were to create a tiered or continuum-based coaching offering (like the Coaching Continuum in Table 8.2), what would it look like? What might be your low-cost or asynchronous entry point? What role could platforms or apps play in your offering?
5. **Act on One Idea**: What is one small, concrete step you could take in the next three months to make your coaching more accessible? This could be a pricing adjustment, a pilot pro-bono programme, or exploring a new platform. Make a note, and a commitment.

Reflect on the quote shared in this chapter, "Who gets threatened most by democracy? It's the people in power". And think how you might begin to share your power as a coach, so coaching can serve not just the few, but the many.

References

Bailey, D., Almusharraf, N., & Hatcher, R. (2021). Finding satisfaction: Intrinsic motivation for synchronous and asynchronous communication in the online language learning context. *Education and Information Technologies*, 26, 2563–2583.

Berry, R. M. (2005). *A comparison of face-to-face and distance coaching practices: The role of the working alliance in problem resolution*. Georgia State University.

Berry, R. M., Ashby, J. S., Gnilka, P. B., & Matheny, K. B. (2011). A comparison of face-to-face and distance coaching practices: Coaches' perceptions of the role of the working alliance in problem resolution. *Consulting Psychology Journal: Practice and Research*, *63*(4), 243.

Boyce, L. A., & Clutterbuck, D. (2010). E-coaching: Accept it, it's here, and it's evolving! In G. Hernez-Broome, L. A. Boyce, & A. I. Kraut (Eds.), *Advancing executive coaching: Setting the course for successful leadership coaching* (pp. 285–315). Wiley.

Charbonneau, M. (2002). *Participant self-perception about the cause of behavior change from a program of executive coaching*. Unpublished doctoral dissertation, Alliant International University, Los Angeles, CA.

Christensen, C. M. (1997). *The innovator's dilemma: When new technologies cause great firms to fail*. Harvard Business School Press.

Dent, E. B., & Goldberg, S. G. (1999). Challenging "resistance to change". *The Journal of Applied Behavioral Science*, *35*(1), 25–41.

Garratt, M., Whiley, L. A., & McDowall, A. (2022). Reflections on video-mediated coaching and a research agenda for coaching psychology. *The Coaching Psychologist*, *18*(1), 6–14.

Gawer, A., & Cusumano, M. A. (2014). Industry platforms and ecosystem innovation. *Journal of Product Innovation Management*, *31*(3), 417–433.
Kanatouri, S. (2020). *The digital coach*. Routledge.
Merron, K. (1993). Let's bury the term "resistance". *Organization Development Journal*, *11*(1), 19–24.
Passarelli, A., Trinh, M. P., Van Oosten, E. B., & Varley, M. (2020). Can you hear me now? The influence of perceived media richness on executive coaching relationships. *Academy of Management Proceedings*, *2020*(1), 20799.
Pfeifer, R., & Scheier, C. (2001). *Understanding intelligence*. MIT Press.
Piderit, S. K. (2000). Rethinking resistance and recognizing ambivalence: A multidimensional view of attitudes toward an organizational change. *Academy of Management Review*, *25*(4), 783–794.
Shoukry, H., & Cox, E. (2018). Coaching as a social process. *Management Learning*, *49*(4), 413–428.

9 New Frameworks, Vocabulary, and Radical Empathy

9.1 What the Coaching Industry Needs to Address

If coaching is to truly serve as a force for human and social transformation, as envisioned in the previous chapter, the responsibility does not rest on individual coaches alone. It extends, indeed, it weighs disproportionately, on the broader ecosystem that shapes how coaching is taught, practised, and accredited. To imagine a democratic, digitally enabled future for coaching is to also confront the question: Is the coaching industry itself ready for that future?

Across the world, industries are recalibrating themselves to meet the demands of digitalisation. Organisations are redesigning their business models; leaders are reimagining their roles; educators are rethinking how learning happens. Yet, the coaching ecosystem, ironically, one that exists to support transformation, appears to be lagging in transforming itself. While executive coaches have begun to experiment with digital tools and hybrid ways of working, coach training institutes, accreditation bodies, and professional associations continue to operate largely within traditional paradigms. The frameworks, competencies, and ethical codes that once shaped the profession's credibility now risk appearing dated in the face of digital disruption.

Part 2 of the book discussed at great length the impact of digitalisation with a coach-centric point of view, but as we all know, unless the ecosystem supports the executive coaches adequately, they are likely to struggle in this journey. If the coaching industry aspires to remain relevant, it must recognise that digitalisation is not an external force acting upon it but an intrinsic part of the environment it now inhabits. This demands more than technical adaptation; it calls for a deeper re-examination of purpose, pedagogy, and practice.

Drawing from the insights of the *4-Winged Framework©*, coach education and accreditation need to move beyond procedural

DOI: 10.4324/9781003638834-13

assessments and consider the deeper dimensions of how coaches **encounter, experience, feel, and respond** to digitalisation. For instance, coach training programmes could explicitly explore how digital tools reshape relational depth and presence (as discussed in Chapter 4), or how emerging technologies like AI might alter the coach's sense of professional identity (as seen in Chapter 6). Similarly, accreditation bodies must revisit their evaluation criteria to include digital fluency, ethical engagement with technology, and the ability to work effectively across virtual and hybrid environments.

To remain static while the world transforms around it is to risk irrelevance. The same digital forces that have disrupted leadership, education, and healthcare will soon test the assumptions underpinning coach education and practice. It would be naïve to assume that an industry built on human connection is somehow immune to technological change. In fact, as we have seen throughout this book, digitalisation need not erode the human essence of coaching, it can amplify it, provided the ecosystem evolves with clarity and courage.

The challenge before the profession, then, is not merely one of adaptation but of stewardship. Those who design training programmes and accreditation standards must now serve as stewards of coaching's future, ensuring that its principles remain timeless even as its practices become timely. The opportunity is immense: to redesign coach education that prepares coaches not just to survive in the digital age, but to thrive as reflective, ethical, and creative practitioners within it.

A shared language, lexicon, and conceptual framework form the foundation of any profession's collective understanding. Without them, it becomes difficult to think, talk, or act coherently about change. The coaching profession is no exception. To navigate the multifaceted and transformative landscape of digitalisation, coaches, and those who train, accredit, and regulate them, need a common vocabulary that can hold both complexity and clarity. Many coaches in my study struggled to articulate what digitalisation truly means for their work. One of them voiced this frustration succinctly: "Digital is something which, in my view, is so poorly defined, there is no standard definition". This lack of definition extends beyond individual practitioners; it reflects a systemic gap. Without a shared conceptual base or agreed frameworks, both coaching practitioners and researchers will continue to struggle to engage with digitalisation in a meaningful, structured way.

This is where the responsibility of coach training institutions and professional accreditation bodies becomes paramount. They must now take the lead in giving coaching a language fit for its digital future, a way to describe and make sense of how technology is reshaping presence, relationship, learning, and practice. The frameworks presented in this book, such as the Nested Framework©, the 4-Winged Framework© and the Coaching Continuum Framework©, offer starting points for such meaning-making. They provide scaffolds for understanding how digitalisation impacts coaching directly and indirectly, helping coaches locate themselves within this evolving context. The very act of naming and framing, however provisional, grants both trainers and practitioners the agency to respond thoughtfully rather than react defensively. These frameworks function as maps. For the coaching profession, such maps can provide orientation amid uncertainty, allowing coach educators, supervisors, and accrediting bodies to design curricula and standards that are not only relevant but forward-looking.

Given the far-reaching effects of digitalisation, as encountered, experienced, and felt by executive coaches, it is essential that training and accreditation bodies embed these frameworks into their dialogue and design. Doing so would enable the broader coaching community to engage more confidently and coherently with digital transformation, ensuring that the profession not only keeps pace with the changing world but helps shape it.

9.2 Defining and Constructing Digital Presence

As the coaching profession steps into its digital future, two dimensions stand out as requiring immediate attention from every stakeholder in the coaching ecosystem: **digital presence** and **greater empathy**. While many other aspects of digital transformation will evolve organically over time, these two demand conscious, urgent action. We next discuss the challenges surrounding digital presence (first introduced in Section 4.2).

Coach training institutions need to help emerging coaches build digital fluency, not just in tools, but in presence, so they can sustain human connection across virtual interfaces. Accreditation bodies must update standards and competency frameworks to recognise digital presence as an essential capability rather than a peripheral skill. Coaching supervisors and mentors must learn to discern and nurture this new form of presence in reflective practice. Organisations and buyers of coaching must evaluate digital coaching offerings not only for convenience and cost, but also for depth, trust, and relational quality. Finally, practising coaches themselves carry the deepest responsibility, to adapt their craft so that technology becomes a bridge, not a barrier, and to bring empathy even more deliberately into a space where physical cues and emotional textures can easily be lost.

Early studies from the pandemic period give a sense of the scale of the disruption in presence. Jarosz (2021) found that working from home introduced an entirely new set of challenges for both coaches and clients, from maintaining productivity while caring for family members to dealing with inadequate technology and unsuitable physical setups. What seemed like mundane inconveniences, an uncomfortable chair, a shaky internet connection, a background noise, often interacted with deeper issues of mental health and emotional fatigue (Williams & Palmer, 2020). For executive coaches, whose practice depends on attention, focus, and a strong working alliance, these disruptions were far from trivial.

These insights resonate deeply with the findings of my own study, where coaches report struggling to re-establish presence in a setting stripped of its familiar rituals. Coaches speak of a "disturbance in the energy space", a "numbing of intuition", "glitch in the matrix", or, as one described it, "the bath water felt just a little bit cold".

Scholars have long emphasised the centrality of presence to coaching effectiveness (De Haan, 2011; De Haan et al., 2011, 2016; Greenson, 1965; O'Neill, 2007, 2011; O'Neill et al., 2005). Theories of working alliance, first developed in psychotherapy (McKenna & Davis, 2009) and later adapted to coaching (De Haan et al., 2011, 2016), link coaching outcomes closely to the coach's psychological and relational presence. Few scholars have since proposed a presence-centred approach for coaches to address precisely the challenges of the digital era.

In my study, coaches described difficulty managing their presence online, missing the physicality of the room, the subtle pacing of dialogue, and the immediacy of shared silence. Those working from relational, somatic, or psychoanalytic orientations felt this loss most acutely, describing how digital mediation muted their sensory awareness and disrupted intuitive flow. For them, digital coaching felt, as one coach said, "like working in a non-native language".

McLaughlin's (2013) proposition, that digital presence should be understood as inherently different rather than deficient, offers a useful way forward. Learning to coach online may indeed resemble learning a new language: awkward at first, but increasingly natural with practice. As with language learning, fluency brings with it new possibilities for expression and connection. Over time, as coaches grow more comfortable in digital spaces, their "inner language of thought", begins to adapt as well.

Recognising digital presence as distinct rather than derivative offers important advantages. It allows coaches to address the unique relational, psychological, and logistical challenges of online work consciously and skilfully. For the broader ecosystem, it creates a shared vocabulary to support training, supervision, and professional standards. Coach training institutes, therefore, need to move beyond treating digital delivery as an optional skill and begin embedding it into their pedagogy as a core competency. Professional bodies can play an enabling role by setting guidelines and ethical standards, much as the UK Council for Psychotherapy (UKCP, 2021) has done for online practice.

The UKCP guidelines explicitly acknowledge that digital environments affect presence and behaviour. Drawing on Suler's (2004) concept of the *online disinhibition effect*, they caution that clients may disclose more freely, express emotion differently, or demonstrate altered patterns of resistance and defence. Such disinhibition can create both opportunities and risks. Coaches who understand these dynamics can respond with attunement, pacing more carefully, listening more deeply, and using silence with greater intentionality. As one coach advised, "Don't go in wham, begin slowly and more gently".

These insights point to an urgent need for the coaching community to articulate its own principles for digital presence. Training programmes must teach future coaches to *design* digital environments consciously, considering light, posture, background, and rhythm as extensions of their relational presence. Supervisors must help practitioners reflect on how their energy translates through a screen. And accreditation bodies must embed digital presence as a recognised marker of professional mastery, not merely an adaptation to circumstance. The adjacent field of psychotherapy has already demonstrated that thoughtful adaptation is possible. For coaching, this moment represents both a challenge and an opportunity: to define what presence means in the digital age, and to ensure that, even through the mediation of screens, the coaching relationship remains a space of deep attention, trust, and transformation.

9.3 The Need for Radical Empathy

None of what we have discussed so far, digital presence, conscious use of technology, or even the evolution of the coaching profession, will be possible without empathy. Not the kind of empathy that sits as a well-worn word in coach training manuals, but a deeper, more radical kind, one that must now extend beyond the client to encompass the medium, the moment, and even the machine. Not even the familiar kind that we often describe in coaching literature, but a more radical and system-wide empathy that acknowledges the scale and depth of transformation coaches and clients are currently experiencing.

Addressing the lack of attention accorded to digitalisation as a socio-contextual phenomenon within coaching research, a few emerging studies have begun to explore its technological expressions. These writings focus primarily on the rise of coach-tech platforms (Kanatouri, 2017, 2020), the use of apps and bots (Terblanche, 2020; Terblanche et al., 2022) and the implications of artificial intelligence and machine learning (a rapidly exploding area of research since 2023). While these contributions are valuable, they overlook the human and emotional dimensions of this transformation, the feelings of imagined irrelevance, the dread of obsolescence, and the fear of change that surfaced so clearly in my research.

To address digitalisation as a socio-contextual movement with wide-ranging implications, it is vital first to acknowledge and understand these strong emotions. The findings from this study reveal that executive coaches are not merely adapting to new tools; they are navigating a profound psychological and professional transition. The struggle to understand digitalisation itself, the shifting coaching agenda (both covered in Chapter 3), the challenges of blurred boundaries, disturbed presence and absent physicality (all covered in Chapter 4) and the opportunity of new windows (Chapter 5) collectively reveal the magnitude of this change. Each element, significant on its own, compounds to produce an atmosphere of uncertainty and unease. The resulting experience for many coaches has been one of disorientation and confusion (as covered in Chapter 6).

It is within this context that empathy must take on a new role. Empathy, as traditionally understood in coaching, has focused on the dyadic relationship, the ability of a coach to step into a client's world with curiosity and compassion. While this remains essential, it is no longer sufficient. The profession must now cultivate **radical empathy**, a systemic, multidimensional empathy that extends beyond individual interactions and permeates the entire coaching ecosystem. Training institutions, supervision practices, and accreditation bodies must approach this period of change not with judgment but with understanding, acknowledging that the journey into digital coaching is as much emotional as it is technical. For coach educators, this means creating learning spaces that honour vulnerability and experimentation, allowing emerging coaches to integrate technology without feeling they are abandoning the relational heart of their practice. For supervisors, it calls for facilitating reflective conversations that help practitioners make sense of how their energy, tone, and presence translate through the screen. Accrediting bodies require embedding digital empathy and digital presence as new markers of professional competence.

Empathy has always been at the centre of coaching, it is what allows one human being to truly see another. Yet, in the digital age, empathy must evolve from being a personal attribute to becoming a collective practice. It must expand its gaze to include not only the human-to-human relationship but also the human-to-system relationship: the interface between coach, client, and the technological environment that now mediates their connection. In essence, **radical empathy** is about recognising that the discomfort, fear, and even resistance among coaches are not signs of weakness, but natural responses to deep change.

9.4 Radical Change Through the Lens of Radical Empathy

At one level, the strong emotions of discomfort, fear, and resistance emerging from imagined irrelevance and dreaded obsolescence can be understood as natural human responses to the large-scale transformation driven by digitalisation, a shift not unlike those seen in earlier industrial revolutions (Mhlanga, 2022; Schwab, 2016). Some studies highlight similar emotions of personal fear, uncertainty, and loss of identity that surfaced during the disruption of COVID-19, suggesting these are not simply reactions to new technologies; they are expressions of what it feels like when familiar structures, rhythms, and meanings are unsettled.

From the perspective of change theory, such moments represent **second-order change**, deep, transformational shifts that affect identity, meaning, and belonging (Manuela & Clara, 2003). These differ markedly from first-order or incremental changes, which are easier to accommodate psychologically. Bridges (2009), in his work on transitions, distinguishes between the *situational change* that happens externally and the *psychological transition* that must happen internally if the change is to be sustained. He reminds us that the most difficult part of any change is not what happens outside us but what happens within. Beisser's (2016) paradoxical theory of change goes even further, suggesting that real transformation occurs not by striving to be different, but by fully engaging with and accepting our present experience.

Seen through the lens change theories, the emotions of fear, uncertainty, and disorientation shared by executive coaches in my research are not peripheral, they are central to the process of adaptation. The literature on change consistently distinguishes external, observable shifts and the internal, psychological transformations that accompany them, whether cognitive (Beck, 1970; Ellis & Grieger, 1986) or psychodynamic (Kubler-Ross, 1969; Satir et al., 1991). Managing the external change without attending to these inner processes risks producing compliance rather than commitment, and motion without meaning.

This is precisely where **radical empathy** becomes essential. To manage digitalisation-driven change effectively, the coaching community must not only understand these psychological undercurrents intellectually but *feel* them empathetically, within themselves and within the systems they serve. Change management models emphasise the need to recognise and work with emotions as catalysts of transition (Cameron & Green, 2019). In the same spirit, fully acknowledging and understanding the emotions experienced by executive coaches, as identified in this research, may well be foundational to enabling the profession's own evolution.

Executive coaches, by virtue of their craft, are already attuned to supporting others through transitions. Yet, the irony revealed through my study is striking: those most skilled at guiding transformation in others are now struggling to navigate their own. This paradox does not signal incapacity but rather humanity. It underscores the need for the coaching profession to extend to itself the same empathy, compassion, and reflective inquiry that it so powerfully offers to others. Evaluating the case for radical empathy, an alternative view might suggest that despite the magnitude of this change, coaching as a field has historically demonstrated remarkable adaptability (Koroleva, 2016). Supporting individuals and organisations through transitions lies at its very heart (Bluckert, 2006). From this perspective, digitalisation represents not a crisis of identity but a call to renewal, an opportunity for the coaching profession to embody, once again, the very principles it teaches.

The difference this time lies in the *pace* and *pervasiveness* of change. Digitalisation is not an external trend to be managed; it is an existential condition that touches how coaches connect, perceive, and make meaning. To respond effectively, coaches must not only develop new digital competencies but also cultivate deeper emotional awareness and collective radical empathy. Only then can they move from resistance to engagement, from anxiety to agency, and from individual adaptation to systemic renewal.

This radical empathy is not a soft skill. It is a strategic necessity, one that will determine whether coaching remains a deeply human profession in an increasingly digital world. Without it, the coaching community risks responding to change with fragmentation and defensiveness. With it, we can reimagine coaching as a field that not only adapts to the digital age but leads it with compassion, awareness, and coherence.

9.5 Empathy in the Post-Pandemic Context

The need for a deeper, system-wide empathy gains even greater urgency in the aftermath of the pandemic. The COVID-19 experience was, for many, both a global event and an intensely personal reckoning. Williams and Palmer (2020), in their study on coaching during COVID-19, observed that the pandemic affected individuals in profoundly different ways, often prompting a search for meaning amid uncertainty. Klingenberg suggested that this collective disruption might compel us to reconsider "who we are and what we value" (Politico, 2020).

For executive coaching, this implies a shift in client priorities. Leaders now face not only the operational challenges of managing distributed and hybrid teams but also deeper questions of purpose, empathy, and well-being. Several respondents in this study echoed this sentiment, suggesting that coaching conversations are increasingly moving beyond performance and leadership skills to include themes of simplicity, connection, and health (Palmer et al., 2020). As one coach put it, "We've all learned something so important about humanity, the closeness of death, the shortness of life. I think that's going to impact leadership coaching".

While themes such as well-being and purpose have always been part of a rounded coaching approach, they have historically been seen as peripheral to executive coaching, which traditionally centres on performance, leadership, and career development. These more reflective and existential dimensions are often categorised under life or wellness coaching.

However, the pandemic blurred these boundaries. As a United Nations briefing observed, "the mental health and well-being of whole societies have been severely impacted by this crisis and are a priority to be addressed urgently" (UN, 2020, p. 2). Increasingly, research shows that coaching can play a pivotal role in this domain. Studies have demonstrated that executive coaching can enhance clients' overall well-being, not just their performance (Cavanagh, 2006; Gabriel et al., 2014; Grant, 2020). Recognising this potential, Williams and Palmer (2020) propose a cognitive-behavioural coaching model that invites executive coaches to "explore the client's experience of the COVID-19 pandemic and develop a strategy to facilitate emotional change and hope for the future" (p. 7). This orientation, rooted in empathy, emotional awareness, and meaning-making, marks an evolution in how coaching might respond to the complexities of our time.

Together, these three strands, *The Need for Radical Empathy*, *Understanding Radical Change through the Lens of Radical Empathy*, and *Empathy in the Post-Pandemic Context*—point to a single, urgent conclusion: the digital age asks the coaching community to do more than learn new tools; it asks us to widen our hearts and our systems. The challenge is both practical and existential. Digitalisation has unsettled assumptions about presence, identity, and depth; the pandemic has amplified our shared vulnerability; and coaches now face the task of holding both technical adaptation and deep emotional work at once.

The way forward is neither retreat nor uncritical embrace, but a deliberate, empathic engagement—one that treats empathy as a strategic, systemic capability. The *Nested Framework©*, *4-Winged Framework©* and the *Coaching Continuum©* are offered as practical scaffolds to help make that engagement actionable. Use them alongside the reflective exercises at the end of various chapters: these exercises translate insight into practice, helping coaches, supervisors and educators to locate themselves, test responses, and iterate new ways of working. With radical empathy as our compass, coaching can move from fragmentation to coherence, not merely surviving the digital moment, but leading it with clarity, compassion, and purpose.

Reflective Exercise 9.1 Standing at the Edge, Practising Radical Empathy in a Changing World

The digital age has placed us, as coaches, at the edge of something profoundly new, a moment where the familiar and the unfamiliar coexist, and where empathy must extend beyond the individual to the entire coaching ecosystem. This exercise invites you to pause and reflect on where you stand in this evolving landscape, emotionally, professionally, and relationally.

1. **The Inner Landscape**: Take a quiet moment and ask yourself:
   - What feelings arise in me when I think about digitalisation and its impact on coaching, excitement, anxiety, curiosity, or resistance?
   - Which part of this transition feels most personal to me?
   - What might these emotions be trying to tell me about my readiness, my fears, or my hopes?
2. **The Outer Connection**: Now, shift your gaze outward. Consider your coaching relationships and broader professional community.
   - Where do I see a need for greater empathy, in my clients, peers, institutions, or the systems around me?
   - How might I model radical empathy in my daily practice, not only with my clients but also with technology, with change, and with myself?
3. **The Systemic View**: Reflect on how your coaching practice interacts with the wider ecosystem.
   - How can empathy inform the design of digital coaching spaces, supervision, or learning environments?
   - What would it look like if empathy were built into the very architecture of how we teach, accredit, and evolve as a profession?

4. **Making It Tangible**: Revisit the *Nested Framework©*, *4-Winged Framework©* and the *Coaching Continuum©* from earlier chapters.
   - Which elements of these frameworks resonate with your current experience of change and empathy?
   - How might you use these models to design small, intentional experiments, perhaps a new way to engage with a client digitally, to reflect with a peer, or to shape your own learning journey?
5. **Looking Forward**: Close your reflection with this simple question: "If empathy were my compass, what would be my next small, courageous step?"

Capture your thoughts in your journal, sketchbook, or digital notes. The goal is not to find definitive answers, but to surface awareness, to see where empathy can become both your guide and your method for navigating the future of coaching in the digital age.

Reflective Exercise 9.2 Cultivating Your Digital Presence

As coaching moves deeper into the digital age, presence is no longer confined to the physical room. This reflection invites you to explore how your presence translates across the screen and how you might consciously strengthen it.

1. **Where do you feel most present?** Recall a recent face-to-face and a virtual session. What shifted in your listening, attention, or connection? What aspects of your presence carried through, and what seemed to fade?
2. **Design your digital space**. Treat your virtual setting as intentionally as your physical one. Consider light, camera, posture, and pace. What subtle changes could make your digital room feel more focused, warm, and human?
3. **Sensing energy online**. Think of a time you sensed an emotional cue through tone, silence, or rhythm in a virtual session. How did you respond? How might you refine your sensitivity to such signals?
4. **Expressing empathy digitally**. What gestures, words, or rituals help you sustain warmth and safety in a digital medium? How can empathy become your bridge across the screen?

Use this reflection as an ongoing practice, an intentional act of presence. Over time, your *digital presence* will become not a compromise but an authentic extension of your coaching self.

References

Beck, A. T. (1970). Cognitive therapy: Nature and relation to behavior therapy. *Behavior therapy*, *1*(2), 184–200.

Beisser, A. (2016). The paradoxical theory of change. https://gestalt.org/arnie.htm.

Bluckert, P. (2006). *Psychological dimensions of executive coaching*. McGraw-Hill Education.

Bridges, W. (2009). *Managing transitions: Making the most of change*. Da Capo Press.

Brown, B. (2021). *Atlas of the heart: Mapping meaningful connection and the language of human experience*. Random House.

Cameron, E., & Green, M. (2019). *Making sense of change management: A complete guide to the models, tools and techniques of organizational change*. Kogan Page Publishers.

Cavanagh, M. (2006). Mental health issues and challenging clients in executive coaching. In D. R. Stober & A. M. Grant (Eds.), *Evidence-based coaching handbook: Putting best practices to work for your clients* (pp. 21–35). Wiley.

De Haan, E. (2011). *Relational coaching: Journeys towards mastering one-to-one learning*. John Wiley & Sons.

De Haan, E., Culpin, V., & Curd, J. (2011). Executive coaching in practice: What determines helpfulness for clients of coaching? *Personnel Review*, *40*(1), 24–44. doi:10.1108/00483481111095500.

De Haan, E., Grant, A. M., Burger, Y., & Eriksson, P.-O. (2016). A large-scale study of executive and workplace coaching: The relative contributions of relationship, personality match, and self-efficacy. *Consulting Psychology Journal: Practice and Research*, *68*(3), 189–207. doi:10.1037/cpb0000058.

Ellis, A. E., & Grieger, R. M. (1986). *Handbook of rational-emotive therapy*, Vol. 2. Springer.

Gabriel, A. S., Moran, C. M., & Gregory, J. B. (2014). How can humanistic coaching affect employee well-being and performance? An application of self-determination theory. *Coaching: An International Journal of Theory, Research and Practice*, 7(1), 56–73.

Grant, A. M. (2020). A languishing–flourishing model of goal striving and mental health for coaching populations. In S. Palmer & A. Whybro (Eds.), *Coaching researched: A coaching psychology reader* (pp. 65–82). Routledge.

Greenson, R. R. (1965). The working alliance and the transference neurosis. *The Psychoanalytic Quarterly*, *34*(2), 155–181.

Jarosz, J. (2021). The impact of coaching on well-being and performance of managers and their teams during pandemic. *International Journal of Evidence Based Coaching and Mentoring*, *19*(1), 4–27.

Kanatouri, S. (2017). An updated list of coaching-specific online tools. *Digital Coaching*. https://digitalcoachreference.wordpress.com/2017/07/01/an-updated-list-of-coaching-specific-online-tools.

Kanatouri, S. (2020). *The digital coach*. Routledge.

Koroleva, N. (2016). A new model of sustainable change in executive coaching: Coachees' attitudes, required resources and routinisation. *International Journal of Evidence Based Coaching & Mentoring*, *14*(1), 16–30.

Kubler-Ross, E. (1969). *On death and dying*. Macmillan.

Manuela, P. V., & Clara, M. F. (2003). Resistance to change: A literature review and empirical study. *Management Decision*, *41*(2), 148–155.

McKenna, D. D., & Davis, S. L. (2009). Hidden in plain sight: The active ingredients of executive coaching. *Industrial and Organizational Psychology*, *2*(3), 244–260.

McLaughlin, M. (2013). Less is more: The executive coach's experience of working on the telephone. *International Journal of Evidence Based Coaching & Mentoring*, *11*(2), 1–15.

Mhlanga, D. (2022). Stakeholder capitalism, the Fourth Industrial Revolution (4IR), and sustainable development: Issues to be resolved. *Sustainability*, *14*(7), 3902.

O'Neill, M. B. (2007). An ROI method for executive coaching: Have the client convince the coach of the return on investment (with commentary). *Consulting Psychology Journal: Practice and Research*, *59*(1), 40–47.

O'Neill, M. B. (2011). *Executive coaching with backbone and heart: A systems approach to engaging leaders with their challenges*. John Wiley & Sons.

O'Neill, M. B., Slattery, J., & Wilson, V. (2005). Executive coaches converse on clients, colleagues, and careers. *Consulting Psychology Journal: Practice and Research*, *57*(2), 99–109.

Palmer, S., Panchal, S., & O'Riordan, S. (2020). Could the experience of the COVID-19 pandemic have any positive impact on wellbeing? *European Journal of Applied Positive Psychology*, *4*(10), 2397–7116.

Politico (Producer). (2020, June 6). Coronavirus will change the world permanently: Here's how. www.politico.com/news/magazine/2020/03/19/coronavirus-effect-economy-life-society-analysis-covid-135579.

Satir, V., Banmen, J., Gomori, M., & Gerber, J. (1991). *The Satir model: Family therapy and beyond*. Science and Behavior Books.

Schwab, K. (2016). *The fourth industrial revolution*. World Economic Forum.

Suler, J. (2004). The online disinhibition effect. *CyberPsychology & Behavior*, *7*(3), 321–326.

Terblanche, N. (2020). A design framework to create artificial intelligence coaches. *International Journal of Evidence Based Coaching & Mentoring*, *18*(2), 152–165.

Terblanche, N., Molyn, J., De Haan, E., & Nilsson, V. O. (2022). Comparing artificial intelligence and human coaching goal attainment efficacy. *PloS One*, *17*(6), e0270255.

UKCP. (2021). UK Council for Psychotherapy guidelines for working online/remotely. www.psychotherapy.org.uk/media/jrohoner/ukcp-guidelines-for-working-online-or-remotely-v1-0.pdf.

UN. (2020). Policy brief: COVID-19 and the need for action on mental health. www.un.org/sites/un2.un.org/files/un_policy_brief-covid_and_mental_health_final.pdf.

Williams, H., & Palmer, S. (2020). Coaching during the COVID-19 pandemic: Application of the CLARITY solution-focused cognitive behavioural coaching model. *International Journal of Evidence Based Coaching and Mentoring*, *18*(2), 204–214.

Part 4

Reflections and Continuing Conversations

10 Reflections, Contributions, and Road Ahead

Every research journey eventually circles back to its starting question,not as a point of closure, but as a deeper return. In the preceding chapters, we have travelled through the terrain of digitalisation as lived and felt by executive coaches: its disruptions, dilemmas, and possibilities. We have seen how new vocabularies, frameworks, and empathic capacities are needed for coaching to remain a human practice in a digital world. Having traced these contours, this chapter now pauses to reflect on what this book has contributed to theory, to practice, and to the broader understanding of coaching as a socio-contextual phenomenon.

To answer the central question—*How are executive coaches dealing with the impact of digitalisation?*—the research required several interlinked lines of inquiry, each addressing a different aspect of how digitalisation is reshaping the field. The journey started with a creative and critical review of the existing literature in executive coaching and digitalisation, along with adjacent helping professions. This exploration, which surfaced key themes around the technological, relational, and human dimensions of digitalisation's influence on practice, has been included in various chapters of this book as academic and theoretical support and informs the discussions of Part 1 of this book. These insights established the intellectual foundation of the research and helped position digitalisation not as an external trend but as a socio-contextual condition that increasingly defines the landscape of coaching itself.

Building on this foundation, the research moved into a deeper investigation of how executive coaches experience, interpret, and respond to digitalisation in their professional lives. Through a systematic exploration of the four conceptual territories, how coaches encounter change, experience loss of depth, imagine irrelevance, and navigate the future (Part 2 of the book), the study revealed how

DOI: 10.4324/9781003638834-15

digitalisation influences the inner and outer worlds of coaching. The findings led to the development of several interrelated frameworks that illuminate this evolving practice. Together, these frameworks offer a cohesive way of understanding how executive coaches engage with the realities of the digital world, how they think about it, feel through it, and act within it. More importantly, they provide the profession with practical and theoretical scaffolds to remain both relevant and deeply human in the digital age.

10.1 Knowledge for Understanding—Contribution to Theory

This section revisits the research objectives and examines how the book has fulfilled its central aim: to explore how digitalisation shapes the experience, identity, and practice of executive coaches, and answers the central research question of: **How are executive coaches dealing with the impact of digitalisation?** In doing so, it positions the book's contributions to theory, how it extends existing understandings of coaching presence, relational depth, and professional adaptation within a rapidly digitalising context.

The qualitative research informing this book is grounded in a social constructivist paradigm and adopts a constructivist grounded theory approach to generate *knowledge for understanding*, a way of knowing that privileges meaning-making over measurement. Using rich, evidence-based narratives and thick descriptions, the research surfaced the subjective and relational layers through which digitalisation is interpreted and embodied in coaching practice. In doing so, it adds to the leadership, business, and coaching literature by positioning digitalisation as not merely a technological development, but as a socio-contextual phenomenon that is transforming how professional identity, presence, and connection are experienced.

The frameworks emerging from this inquiry, particularly the *Nested Framework©*, the *4-Winged Framework for Coaching in the Digital Age©* (Chapter 7), and the *Coaching Continuum©* (Chapter 9), contribute to theoretical understanding by introducing digitalisation as an integral context for coaching theory. These frameworks address a long-standing gap in coaching scholarship, which has often treated practice as context-neutral and underexplored the systemic and socio-technical influences shaping it. By situating digitalisation alongside established theories of learning and change, this book proposes a more holistic way of viewing the coaching process, one that acknowledges how technological, relational, and emotional dimensions interact to shape both coach and client experience. In doing so, it lays the groundwork for future research to explore coaching not just as an interpersonal process, but as a meaning-making system that evolves with its environment.

With the massive and transformational shifts brought by digitalisation in the context of the Fourth Industrial Revolution, executive coaches are being called to learn, unlearn, and adapt continuously if they are to thrive in the digital age. The four-element cycle proposed in the *4-Winged Framework for Coaching in the Digital Age©* can be viewed in conversation with Kolb's experiential learning cycle (Kolb, 2014), which comprises four stages, concrete experience, reflective observation, abstract conceptualisation, and active experimentation. Unlike Kolb's sequential model, however, the elements of the 4-Winged Framework do not follow a fixed order. They unfold in fluid, sometimes recursive ways, reflecting the dynamic and non-linear nature of how coaches encounter and respond to digitalisation. Each coach's journey may take a different route, some moving through all stages, others circling back, skipping steps, or discovering new pathways altogether. While a direct correspondence cannot be claimed, certain resonances can be observed: Kolb's "concrete experience" aligns closely with the *encountering* and *experiencing* elements, "reflective observation" finds echoes in *feeling*, and "active experimentation" in *responding*.

Most current research on digital tools and technologies in coaching remains situated within the logic of behaviourist and cognitive learning theories (Ertmer & Newby, 2013, 2016), where technology is something to be learned *about* or *from*. The findings covered in this book suggest a more nuanced picture. Executive coaches are not passive recipients of change driven by digitalisation; they are active participants in shaping and managing it within their practice. In doing so, they demonstrate self-efficacy (Bandura, 1994), the belief in one's ability to succeed in specific contexts or tasks. To reflect this agency, research and practice in coaching must now move beyond learning *about* technology towards learning *with* technology. Such a stance is consistent with the constructivist and andragogical principles outlined by Knowles (1980), where adults learn best through self-directed, experiential engagement. Integrating these learning theories with coaching practice, as Cox

(2006) has previously advocated, offers a pathway for evolving coaching theory itself, towards one that is both contextually aware and capable of making meaning in the midst of digital transformation.

This book also contributes to the business and leadership literature exploring the impact of digitalisation on teams, leaders, and organisations. The changed coaching agenda of greater empathy suggests that to better understand the impact of forces of digitalisation on teams, leaders, organisations and businesses, the factors of digital presence, along with the feelings and fears of crucial stakeholders, help chart a more informed middle path against the extremes of utopian and dystopian views.

10.2 Knowledge for Action—Contribution to Practice

The previous section explored how this book contributes to *knowledge for understanding*; this section turns to *knowledge for action*, how its insights and frameworks can inform and enrich coaching practice. The discussions throughout this book, coupled with real case studies and reflective exercises at the end of each chapter, offer executive coaches not only conceptual clarity but also a shared vocabulary to engage with the implications of digitalisation in their daily work. By examining how digitalisation reshapes presence, empathy, and the coaching relationship, this book invites practitioners to translate awareness into action, to adapt their methods, refine their presence, and engage more intentionally with the digital environments in which they now work, through the reflective exercises.

As coaching continues to expand across virtual and hybrid spaces, practitioners are seeking clearer guidance on how to sustain quality, depth, and ethics in video-based sessions. In this regard, the practical reflections shared across the chapters align with the kind of considerations outlined by professional bodies such as the UK Council for Psychotherapy (UKCP, 2021), whose guidelines for online work highlight critical issues of security, privacy, and compliance in digital practice. These also note the subtle relational challenges of screen-based communication, for instance, the altered experience of eye contact when cameras are misaligned or the heightened sense of scrutiny created by sustained visual focus. Such details, while seemingly minor, profoundly influence the felt quality of presence between coach and client. This book emphasises that awareness of these nuances—and the ability to consciously design one's digital environment (covered in Chapters 4 and 5).

The *4-Winged Framework for Coaching in the Digital Age©* offers not only a conceptual lens but also a practical vocabulary for coaching supervision. Each of its four elements, and the framework as a whole, creates a structured yet flexible way for supervisors to engage coaches in reflective dialogue about their experiences, fears, and adaptive responses to digitalisation. It enables supervisory conversations to move beyond performance or technique and into the deeper emotional and relational dimensions of digital practice. Within this frame, discussions of empathy, digital presence, and the evolving *Coaching Continuum©* gain greater coherence and depth, allowing supervisors, educators, and professional bodies to collectively nurture a generation of coaches who are both technologically fluent and emotionally attuned. This, forms an essential part of a coach's professional competence in the digital age.

Looking ahead, the frameworks and themes discussed throughout this book also open new avenues for coaching researchers. As virtual interactions continue to grow across industries and cultures in the post-pandemic world, the effectiveness and ethics of coaching through digital interfaces will likely attract increasing scholarly attention. The Coaching Continuum Framework© provides an orienting scaffold for such inquiry, offering variables and dimensions that researchers can test, adapt, or expand as the field matures. For practitioners, the same continuum offers a map for experimentation: a way to navigate the expanding landscape of digital tools and interfaces while remaining anchored in reflective, human-centred practice. In this sense, the book contributes both to *knowledge for action* and to the ongoing evolution of *knowledge about action*, bridging practice, supervision, and future research in a shared conversation about what it means to coach in the digital age.

In summary, this book suggests that executive coaches must now see the management of virtual sessions and the cultivation of digital presence as central to their craft. Many of the coaches who participated in this study, and whose experiences have informed the reflections in this book, were themselves experimenting, often for the first time, with ways of building presence, depth, and connection through a screen. Their practices were evolving in real time, shaped by trial, curiosity, and reflection. This spirit of ongoing experimentation is likely to remain essential as the profession continues to adapt to emerging technologies and new relational forms. Over time, these learnings will need to find their way into coach education, supervision, and accreditation, ensuring that digital presence and empathy become integral to how coaching is taught and practised. As one participant insightfully remarked, "This virtual coaching, the craft of it, the art of it, the skill of it, etcetera, as a teachable piece, still needs to be developed".

10.3 Limitations of the Research and the Book

Coaching in the digital age, as explored throughout this book, emerges as both an evolving practice and an unfinished conversation. While the discussions and frameworks presented here offer meaningful insights into how executive coaches are encountering and adapting to digitalisation, they also open up new questions. There is still much to understand about how coaches learn, sustain presence, and reimagine connection in digitally mediated spaces, and about how institutions, educators, and professional bodies can support that evolution. This section acknowledges the limitations of this research and of the book itself, while pointing towards directions for future inquiry that can continue to deepen and expand our collective understanding of coaching in a rapidly digitalising world.

Like any qualitative inquiry, this research, and by extension, this book, carries inherent limitations arising from its methodological choices. These include the relatively small and context-specific sample, the potential influence of researcher subjectivity, and the limited generalisability of findings beyond comparable settings. Rooted in an interpretivist paradigm, the study privileges depth of understanding over breadth of coverage; its insights are therefore best read within the boundaries of the context in which they were generated (Saunders & Thornhill, 2019). The findings represent meaning as constructed and shared by participants rather than as universal truths (Crotty, 1998). Additionally, the temporal context of the research, the period shaped by the global COVID-19 pandemic, inevitably influenced both participants and the researcher. The pandemic served as both backdrop and catalyst, amplifying many of the themes explored in this book, particularly those relating to presence, empathy, and adaptation. Future studies conducted in different conditions may therefore surface new or evolving perspectives as the coaching profession continues to mature in its digital practice.

The social constructivist foundation of this research also recognises the inherent limits of sense-making. The multiple perspectives and interpretations presented here are best understood as constructions of reality, shaped by the lived experiences, values, and beliefs of both the respondents and the researcher. Meaning, in this view, is always situated and partial, never final or universal. Consequently, any attempt to extend or generalise the insights of this book beyond the context in which they were developed must be approached with care and reflexivity. Furthermore, as with any interpretive study, the findings are influenced by the way the central question was framed and by the specific methodological choices made to explore it. These boundaries do not diminish the value of the work; rather, they highlight the interpretive and evolving nature of knowledge in a field as dynamic and context-dependent as coaching in the digital age.

The composition of respondents and their demographic profile, which are shared in the Appendix, present additional limitations for both the research and this book. The insights discussed here are drawn from the perspectives of executive coaches based primarily in the United Kingdom, Germany, the United States, India, and South Africa. Coaches working in other regions, particularly those at different stages of digital adoption or operating within distinct cultural and economic contexts, may well experience digitalisation in ways that differ from those captured in this study. Furthermore, the participants in this research were all senior practitioners with substantial coaching experience. Their depth of reflection and maturity of practice offered rich insight into the profession's evolution, but a younger or less experienced cohort might reveal alternate narratives, perhaps marked by different expectations, comfort levels, and creative approaches to technology. Future research that includes a broader and more diverse range of voices may therefore provide a diverse and differently nuanced picture of how digitalisation is reshaping coaching across generations, geographies, and practice settings.

As with all social constructivist grounded theory studies, this work carries the challenge of generating interpretations that remain faithful to the respondents' lived realities while being mindful of the researcher's own influence. The insights presented here are therefore inevitably shaped, to some degree, by my own beliefs, values, and presuppositions. These have been made explicit throughout the book, and deliberate efforts were taken during research to mitigate their undue impact by continually comparing data with data, allowing patterns and categories to emerge from within the participants' accounts rather than from my assumptions (Charmaz, 2014). Nonetheless, in an interpretive paradigm such as this, complete neutrality is neither possible nor desirable. Knowledge is always co-created between researcher and participants, and meaning evolves through dialogue rather than discovery. It is therefore reasonable to expect that another researcher, working with the same data, might make different interpretive choices and arrive at alternate yet equally valid understandings of how digitalisation is shaping executive coaching.

In closing, while every effort has been made to ensure rigour and reflexivity, this research inevitably carries the interpretive boundaries discussed above. It also draws upon theories from adjacent disciplines, learning, change, technology, and human–AI interaction, to enrich understanding of coaching in the digital age. Yet, the fast-evolving nature of digitalisation presents its own challenge. The pace of advancement, particularly in artificial intelligence and machine learning, continues to outstrip the timeline of any single inquiry. For instance, during the preparation of the final draft of my thesis (October 2022 – March 2023), the launch of OpenAI's ChatGPT dramatically expanded the capabilities of conversational AI through the integration of deep learning and large language models. This also influenced me to add an Afterword in this book, where I specifically discuss the emergence of conversational AI. Such developments remind us that the landscape explored in this book is not static but unfolding—inviting ongoing research, reflection, and dialogue as coaching continues to evolve within this dynamic digital frontier.

10.4 Directions for Future Research

Looking ahead, future research will need to extend the inquiry into new dimensions of digitalisation and coaching. To build a more comprehensive understanding of how digital transformation is reshaping the coaching ecosystem, it is essential to include the perspectives of multiple stakeholders beyond the coach. These would include clients, supervisors, coach training institutions, organisational sponsors, and professional bodies, each offering distinct yet interconnected insights into how digitalisation influences coaching relationships and outcomes. Expanding the scope of participants in this way could lead to a broader research question: *How is digitalisation impacting the various stakeholders of executive coaching?*

Such an exploration would be particularly valuable in understanding, for instance, how clients experience "loss of depth" or "disturbed presence", or how organisations perceive shifts in value and effectiveness as coaching moves increasingly into digital spaces. For constructivist researchers, where meaning is co-created through participants' interpretations, engaging a wider range of voices could further enrich the understanding of the Coaching Continuum© proposed in this book.

The findings discussed in this book, together with emerging research in human–automation interaction (HAI), indicate that individual differences, such as personality traits and attitudes towards technology, may play a significant role in how executive coaches integrate digital tools and platforms into their practice. Future research could usefully examine how personality influences this process, drawing on established frameworks such as the Big Five model or newer conceptualisations of personality in digital contexts (Feher & Vernon, 2021). This line of inquiry might be framed around the question: *How does the personality of executive coaches shape the adoption and use of emerging digital tools?* Such exploration would not only deepen our understanding of individual adaptation but also illuminate how personal dispositions intersect with professional identity, learning preferences, and technological fluency. Viewing HAI through an interdisciplinary lens thus opens rich possibilities for coaching researchers, to explore how coaches can learn *with* technology, rather than merely *about* it, and to advance more integrated models of human–digital collaboration in coaching.

The findings of this book highlight that the emergence of new virtual spaces has opened an important frontier for further research and dialogue in coaching. Many coaches are seeking guidance on how to navigate and sustain presence within these digitally mediated environments. The study suggests that *digital presence* must be recognised as a distinct construct, one that warrants deeper exploration to understand how coaches can consciously cultivate it to hold virtual space more effectively and to foster empathetic, meaningful connections with clients. Future inquiry could therefore examine questions such as: *How does digitalisation influence the presence of coaches and clients in virtual settings?* Addressing this would not only expand theoretical understanding but also inform practical approaches for training and supervision, helping the profession strengthen its capacity for human connection in an increasingly digital world.

To conclude, it may be fitting to suggest that, given the limitations of this study and the many avenues for future inquiry, continued exploration of how digitalisation is reshaping executive coaching will be both necessary and rewarding for the field. The questions raised in this book and the new research questions suggested in this section are invitations to study more deeply, to listen more widely, and to remain curious about how technology continues to transform what it means to connect, learn, and grow as human beings. In many ways, the journey of coaching in the digital age mirrors the journey of knowledge itself: cyclical, unfolding, and ever-renewing. As T. S. Eliot reminds us in *Little Gidding*, "We shall not cease from exploration, and the end of all our exploring will be to arrive where we started and know the place for the first time" (1943). This spirit of exploration, humble, reflective, and enduring, perhaps best captures the work that lies ahead for coaching as it continues to evolve in the digital age.

10.5 Personal Reflection—The Researcher's Journey

Lewis (2005) suggests that what one sees and hears depends a great deal on where one is standing. Like many researchers, I began this inquiry with a set of ontological and epistemological assumptions, beliefs that quietly informed how I made sense of the world, but which had rarely been tested or named. The early stages of this research and the process of writing this book offered an unanticipated invitation to examine those foundations with honesty and curiosity. The period of my research and writing of the thesis became a journey of philosophical discovery as much as academic exploration. As I engaged with different paradigms and perspectives, I found myself questioning not just how I was researching, but who I was becoming in the process. There were moments of disorientation and self-doubt, periods when the ground beneath my intellectual footing seemed to shift completely. Sometimes, researchers and first-time authors must first be thoroughly lost before they can truly find their way. I came to understand and even embrace this "lostness" as a necessary part of my own transformation.

Early in my research journey, it became clear that as I transitioned into the dual identity of a relational coach and a researching professional, the positivist foundations of my engineering education and corporate experience no longer served me well. Yet, it was only when I was deep into writing the methodology chapter of my thesis, constantly challenged and supported by my supervisory team, that I began to find more solid ground within the interpretive perspective and the social constructivist paradigm.

Throughout this research and the writing of this book, I remained conscious of my multiple identities as a senior organisational leader, a researcher, an internal executive coach, and an author, roles that inevitably shaped my perspective during the research and writing of this book. Passmore and Fillery-Travis (2011) encourage coaching researchers to transcend the traditional practitioner–academic divide and embrace the identity of a *researching practitioner*. I found this integrative stance both affirming and liberating. Rather than viewing my professional experience as a challenge, I came to see it as a vital lens through which to interpret the realities of digitalisation. As an internal coach working within a technology-driven organisation and leading digital transformation for over a decade, I have witnessed first-hand the profound shifts that technology has brought to leadership, learning, and human connection. Acknowledging this position, neither detached observer nor wholly embedded participant, helped me situate my reflections with greater clarity. And, after finishing my research, these identities inspired me to write this book, which can reach a larger audience and hopefully impact the coaching industry and its many stakeholders constructively. I hope that by making this stance transparent, readers can better appreciate the context in which this work was conceived and assess its insights with an informed understanding of the perspective from which they emerged.

While I take great pride in the knowledge this book contributes to the field of executive coaching, I am equally grateful for the process of finding my own presence and philosophical footing, and for how that search, through both the research and the writing of this book, has shaped me as a person, an author, and a professional researcher. I have come to feel an increasing ease in describing my conclusions as *provisional*, *tentative*, and *evolving*, and in seeing this work as one possible construction of knowledge among many others. In that realisation, I no longer view myself as a detached observer but as a seeking subject, both shaped by and shaping the very inquiry I have pursued. The following quotation captures this stance and the quiet sense of alignment I now feel with my philosophical home.

> Within infinite myths lies the eternal truth.
>
> Who sees it all?
>
> Varuna [the God of Wind] has but a thousand eyes, Indra [the King of Gods] has a hundred,
>
> You and I only two.
>
> (Pattnaik, 2016)

My presence in coaching conversations, and in life, continues to shape, make, and move each encounter. As a coach, I strive to use the *self as an instrument of change* (Seashore et al., 2004), placing the client's needs at the centre while remaining aware of how my own experiences, beliefs, and assumptions influence the space we share. Writing this book has deepened that awareness. It has invited me to see my coaching sessions not merely as structured dialogues, but as *conversational, reflexive inquiries*, living exchanges where meaning is co-created in the moment. In many ways, the process of writing mirrored the act of coaching itself: iterative, uncertain, and profoundly relational.

Through the writing of this book, I have become more attentive to my own presence, how it enters a room, shapes a question, or shifts an emotional undercurrent. It has helped me listen with greater curiosity, hold ambiguity with more ease, and bring a quieter humility to the practice of coaching. If, in some small way, these reflections and frameworks help readers experience a similar deepening in their own presence and practice, then this journey will have served its purpose.

References

Bandura, A. (1994). Self-efficacy. In V. S. Ramachaudran (Ed.), *Encyclopedia of human behavior* (Vol. 4, pp. 71–81). Academic Press.

Charmaz, K. (2014). *Constructing grounded theory*. Sage.

Cox, E. (2006). An adult learning approach to coaching. In D. R. Stober & A. M. Grant (Eds.), *Evidence-based coaching handbook* (pp. 193–217). Wiley.

Crotty, M. (1998). *The foundations of social research: Meaning and perspective in the research process*. Sage.

Eliot, T. S. (1943). *Little gidding*. Faber & Faber.

Ertmer, P. A., & Newby, T. J. (2013). Behaviorism, cognitivism, constructivism: Comparing critical features from an instructional design perspective. *Performance Improvement Quarterly*, 26(2), 43–71.

Ertmer, P. A., & Newby, T. J. (2016). Learning theory and technology: A reciprocal relationship. In D. S. N. Rushby (Ed.), *The Wiley handbook of learning technology*. John Wiley & Sons.

Feher, A., & Vernon, P. A. (2021). Looking beyond the Big Five: A selective review of alternatives to the Big Five model of personality. *Personality and Individual Differences*, *169*, 110002.

Knowles, M. S. (1980). *The modern practice of adult education: From pedagogy to andragogy* (Rev. and updated ed.). Association Press. (Original work published 1970).

Kolb, D. A. (2014). *Experiential learning: Experience as the source of learning and development*. FT Press.

Lewis, C. S. (2005). *The magician's nephew*. Zondervan.

Passmore, J., & Fillery-Travis, A. (2011). A critical review of executive coaching research: A decade of progress and what's to come. *Coaching: An International Journal of Theory, Research and Practice*, *4*(2), 70–88.

Pattnaik, D. (2016). *Myth = mithya: A handbook of Hindu mythology*. Penguin.

Saunders, L. P., & Thornhill, A. (2019). *Research methods for business students*. Pearson Education.

Seashore, C., Shawver, M., Thompson, G., & Mattare, M. (2004). Doing good by knowing who you are. *OD Practitioner*, *36*(3), 42–46.

UKCP. (2021). UK Council for Psychotherapy guidelines for working online/remotely. www.psychotherapy.org.uk/media/jrohoner/ukcp-guidelines-for-working-online-or-remotely-v1-0.pdf.

Afterword

Generative AI and Conversations

In the 21st century, change has become so relentless that the phrase *accelerating change* now feels almost cliché in social and management literature,yet its truth is undeniable. During the course of my research and thesis writing (2018–2023), the world lived through a deadly pandemic that upended economies and lives, witnessed the swift development of a global vaccine, and saw the outbreak of war in Ukraine, which reshaped global food and energy systems. Even as I crafted this book, the world remained in motion: a new US presidency triggered tariff shifts and trade tensions, while devastating conflicts in the Middle East deepened geopolitical instability. At the same time, intensifying climate crises and extreme weather events have continued to expose the urgency of sustainable action.

Against this backdrop, the inclusion of this afterword is prompted by another consequential development,not as catastrophic as a pandemic, war, or climate breakdown, yet one that may prove equally transformative for human society and the ecosystems we inhabit.

A Turning Point in Time: In October 2022, I completed my research that underpins this book. One month later, the world met *ChatGPT*.

The coincidence of these two moments felt symbolic, an ending that immediately opened into a new beginning. While my research had explored digitalisation as a profound socio-contextual force transforming executive coaching, the release of conversational AI marked the arrival of something even more intimate: technology capable not only of *mediating* dialogue but possibly *participating* in it.

The launch of OpenAI's ChatGPT in November 2022, followed rapidly by responses from Google, Meta, and others, heralded a new chapter in human–machine interaction. These large language models can generate text, simulate tone, and sustain contextual conversations with remarkable coherence. Within months, they moved from being

DOI: 10.4324/9781003638834-16

technological curiosities to everyday companions, collaborators, and, in some cases, advisors.

The acceleration is breath-taking, yet it is not without precedent. The history of human–machine dialogue stretches back decades, and the seeds of today's conversational AI were sown long before ChatGPT ever spoke its first word.

ELIZA and the Origins of Machine Conversations: In 1966, Joseph Weizenbaum, a computer scientist at MIT, created ELIZA—a program designed to mimic a Rogerian psychotherapist by rephrasing users' inputs as reflective questions (Weizenbaum, 1966). Weizenbaum's intent was satirical; he sought to demonstrate the superficiality of machine conversation. But what followed astonished him. Users began to disclose personal feelings and private confessions to the program. Some even requested that others leave the room so they could "speak to ELIZA alone". What was meant as a parody became a mirror, revealing not the machine's intelligence but the human longing for empathy, recognition, and response. Weizenbaum was unsettled by this discovery and spent the rest of his career warning of the ethical dangers of granting computers too much emotional authority. Yet his creation revealed something essential about human nature: our instinct to seek understanding, even in coded reflection.

That paradox, the shallow script evoking deep emotion, remains alive today. It suggests that technology, however mechanical, becomes a canvas for projection. People do not merely *use* tools like ChatGPT; they enter into a kind of relationship with them. And it is within that relationship that coaching, once again, finds itself at a fascinating threshold.

A Continuum, Not a Break: It might be tempting to view the emergence of conversational AI as a rupture, a sudden leap into a post-human future. Yet, in truth, it represents continuity rather than discontinuity. Digitalisation and AI are threads of the same tapestry, woven together through the ongoing evolution of human communication.

The questions this book has explored, how coaches *encounter* change, *experience* loss of depth, *imagine* irrelevance, and *respond* creatively, remain equally relevant, perhaps even more so, in the age of Generative AI. The *4-Winged Framework for Coaching in the Digital Age©* and the *Coaching Continuum©* could easily be revisited by substituting "digitalisation" with "conversational AI", or even "ChatGPT".

For the coaching profession, this new era calls not for alarm, but for inquiry. We must now study not only *how* coaches use AI, but also *how AI changes the experience of coaching itself*. Does it expand human potential, or subtly reshape it? Does it amplify empathy, or simulate it? This work also invites interdisciplinary exploration, drawing from fields like HAI, psychology, and learning theory, to understand how meaning, identity, and emotion evolve when the "other" in the conversation is a machine. Such inquiry is not simply technical, it is philosophical. It asks us to reflect once again on the boundaries of knowing, presence, and humanity itself.

The Human Thread—What Remains Timeless: Despite the pace of technological advancement, certain truths endure. Coaching, at its heart, remains a profoundly human act—rooted in empathy, presence, and curiosity. These qualities cannot be replicated by code, only simulated. Machines can generate empathy-like responses, but only humans can mean them. The emergence of conversational AI challenges us not to compete with technology, but to deepen what is uniquely ours. The more sophisticated the tools become, the more essential it is for coaches to cultivate the qualities that cannot be automated: listening with full attention, holding silence with compassion, and co-creating meaning with humility.

In this sense, the human element does not diminish in the age of AI, it becomes even more vital. As one might say, the light of empathy shines brighter when cast against the glow of the machine.

Continuing the Conversation: The appearance of ChatGPT and its successors marks a profound inflexion point, but also a reminder that technological progress is never the whole story. Each innovation reopens timeless questions: What does it mean to understand another person? To listen, to connect, to change? As this book closes, I return to the spirit that animated its beginning, the belief that coaching, at its best, is a human dialogue in times of radical change. Digitalisation and AI may alter the medium of that dialogue, but not its essence.

In the end, perhaps the real question is not whether machines can think, but whether we will continue to. Whether, amid our tools and technologies, we can stay in touch with the pulse of presence, the fragility of empathy, and the enduring art of being human.

The conversation, like coaching itself, continues.

> We shape our tools and thereafter our tools shape us.
>
> (Hurme & Jouhki, 2017)

References

Hurme, P., & Jouhki, J. (2017). We shape our tools, and thereafter our tools shape us. *Human Technology*, *13*(2), 145–148.

Weizenbaum, J. (1966). ELIZA—a computer program for the study of natural language communication between man and machine. *Communications of the ACM*, *9*(1), 36–45.

Appendix

Details of My Respondents

Pseudonym	*Gender*	*Age Range*	*Country*	*Profile*	
Ganga	F	50–55	**India**	Part Owner	Executive Coaching, Leadership Development and Facilitation
Garima	M	50–55	**India**	Consultant	Executive Coaching, Leadership Development
Kylie	F	45–50	**UK**	Own Company	Executive Coaching
Paul	M	50–55	**UK**	Fin Tech	Executive & Board Coaching
Michael	M	45–50	**Germany**	Own Company	Executive Coaching
Willow	F	65–70	**UK**	Part Owner	Executive Coaching, HR Consulting
Amber	F	65–70	**USA**	Part Owner	Executive Coaching, Leadership Development
Caleb	M	45–50	**UK**	Part Owner	Executive & Team Coach, Supervision & Organisation Design Consulting
Prakash	M	60–65	**India**	Freelancer	Executive Coaching & HR Consulting
Nikhil	M	60–65	**India**	Part Owner	Executive Coaching & Organisational Consulting
Leah	F	45–50	**UK**	Own Company	Executive Coaching
Sanjay	M	50–55	**India**	Consulting	Executing Coaching & HR Consulting
Anil	M	70–75	**India**	Part Owner	Executive Coaching & Leadership Development
Rohan	M	70–75	**India**	Own Company	Executive Coaching, Supervision, Leadership Development
Flora	F	45–50	**USA**	Consulting	Executive Coaching & HR Consulting

(*Continued*)

Pseudonym	*Gender*	*Age Range*	*Country*	*Profile*	
Bhavesh	M	55–60	**India**	Own Company	Executive Coaching, Supervision & Leadership Development
Gloria	F	50–55	**UK**	Own Company	Executive Coaching, Leadership Development and Facilitation
Brian	M	60–65	**UK**	Associate	Executive Coach, Supervision & Psychotherapist
Daniel	M	45–50	**UK**	Part Owner	Executive Coach, Psychologist, Change Consultant
Aaron	M	45–50	**UK**	Part Owner	Executive Coach, Psychologist, Change Consultant
Keith	M	50–55	**UK**	Freelancer	Executive Coach, Consultant
Bhumi	F	50–55	**India**	Own Company	Executive Coach & Leadership Development
Caleb	M	50–55	**UK**	Own Company	Executive Coaching, Leadership Development and Facilitation
Divya	F	45–50	**USA**	Consulting	Executive Coaching & HR Consulting
Eshwar	M	50–55	**India**	Part Owner	Executive Coach & Leadership Development

Index

Note to index: page numbers in *italics* refer to information in figures; page numbers in **bold** refer to information in tables.

For Product Safety Concerns and Information please contact our EU
representative GPSR@taylorandfrancis.com
Taylor & Francis Verlag GmbH, Kaufingerstraße 24, 80331 München, Germany

www.ingramcontent.com/pod-product-compliance
Lightning Source LLC
LaVergne TN
LVHW010901110826
845149LV00005B/1433

* 9 7 8 1 0 4 1 0 7 1 0 3 7 *